THE WAC

The Wacky Parts of My Oeuvre

By DAVID FLOWERS

THE WACKY PARTS OF MY OEUVRE

ISBN: 978-1-7338319-3-2

THE WACKY PARTS OF MY OEUVRE

Ignorance of the law excuses no man -- from practicing it.

Italian proverb

ACKNOWLEDGMENTS

I owe debts of gratitude to many who have touched this project along the way.

I am grateful to Lee Plumblee for suggesting that I take on this endeavor many years ago. I also want to thank him for pointing out how boring an earlier draft of this book was. In doing so, he helped make it better.

I am grateful to Natali, my wife for, among many things, taking and then suggesting that I use the photo that is on the cover. She tricked me into posing that way. I had no idea what was on the wall behind me. I think she likes the picture because in her mind, that is how I appear each and every day to everyone who encounters me.

I am grateful to Beck Sipes for doing the graphic design on the front and back covers.

To those who read drafts, I am indebted for your time and valuable feedback. Any mistakes the reader may encounter herein are mine alone.

AUTHOR'S NOTE

My aim in this book is merely to entertain. I do not intend to settle any scores or embarrass anyone (who doesn't deserve to be embarrassed), so I have left out names and identifying information of many of the lawyers and judges and litigants included in these stories.

I chose to begin this collection with stories about the two lawyers who had the most impact on my career because they also appear throughout the book, and I wanted you to get to know them first.

I have included many stories from my career which are funny, weird, or otherwise interesting. I have chosen to not include many other stories. Because of the work I did, many of those other stories are tragic, horrible, and sad. I've lived (and will continue to live) with them long enough. No good purpose would be served by rehashing them here or burdening others with them. So, my hope is that the ones I have chosen to include here will bring a smile, or at least a smirk, to your face.

To anyone and everyone who contributed to me becoming the lawyer I became…

whether intended or not.

FOREWORD

My son is a lawyer. He was admitted to the Bar just this past year and has begun to practice with me. It is a joy and a privilege that was unexpected, as neither of my children ever had expressed an interest in becoming lawyers in their formative years. When my son was in his senior year of college at Clemson (where the author of this book and I both proudly attended), he came to me and told me of his plan to apply to law school. It was difficult to hide my excitement that my own child had experienced at least some remote admiration for his father's profession, but, in all candor, I suspected that this determination to attend law school might just stem from the desire to avoid the real world and to engage in another three years of fully-funded, unsupervised living.

So, I told my son that, while I was thrilled that he was considering joining our profession, I wanted him to give me the reason or reasons behind this decision. I wanted to determine the sincerity of his decision and was willing to use some of the cross-examination techniques that 30-years at the Bar can teach one. His answer surprised and, honestly, delighted me.

First, he said, lawyers, despite the jokes, are respected. They hold positions of leadership not just in the legal world, but in other organizations, being on Boards of Directors of, in some cases, for-profit businesses, in others, non-profit charities. They serve in positions of leadership in politics and in church and other social and fraternal organizations. In short, people look up to them, even when they make fun of them. (This was going better than I had expected).

Next, he said, lawyers generally are comfortably compensated. A law practice isn't a gold mine, he said, but it could be a silver mine if you work hard and manage it well. (Okay, I'll have to admit, he had me at this point. The cross-examination was over, but what I didn't know was that the best was yet to come).

"But the main reason that I want to be a lawyer, Dad," he said, "is that you and your friends just have the best stories."

We trial lawyers are a peculiar lot. We are hired guns, paid to advocate a position for a client against, presumably, an able adversary who is being paid by his or her client to do the same. While most people prefer to avoid conflict, we wallow in it. We get paid for it, and let's just be honest, on some level, we like it. Not because we are particularly contentious people. On the contrary, some of the nicest and most professional people that I ever have met have been my adversaries in the courtroom. In many cases, they have been personal friends. But we still don't want to lose to each other any more than a professional athlete wants to lose the Super Bowl to a friend's team, and we love being in the heat of battle in the courtroom.

Another peculiarity of trial lawyers is that, while most people are prohibited from knowing the private details of the personal lives of others, we get paid to root around in that stuff. It leads to all sorts of interesting, titillating, and appalling discoveries.

And then, of course, there is the fact that trial lawyers are interesting people. From Abe Lincoln to Clarence Darrow to Johnny Cochran and Johnny Hagins, whom you will meet in this book, this profession always has been populated by characters.

When you combine all of this conflict, compensated voyeurism, and shoulder-rubbing with the smartest and most charismatic adversaries on the planet, it can lay the groundwork for some great stories. And trial lawyers love to tell stories. The best venue for good lawyer stories used to be the time between jury charges by the court and verdict, the time during which the jury was deliberating the outcome of your case. There really isn't much to do in this time other than to pace, worry, pace, worry… or tell stories with your opponent. The stories beat the pacing and worrying without question. Regrettably, the civil jury trial, for many reasons which would take too long to explain here, has gone more-or-less the way of the dinosaurs and the rotary telephone. There just are very few cases being tried these days. We trial lawyers must be content to see one another now in depositions, in court-ordered mediations, or at professional functions which, thankfully, usually involve open bars, a stimulus which not only encourages good story-telling, but which liberates it from the unreasonable restrictions of actual factual support. (It is a bit like being the President of the United States in these most modern times, except that lawyer stories do contain *some* elements of genuine fact.)

My fascination with stories began long before I was a lawyer. I grew up in the country, next door to my maternal grandparents. My mother's maternal grandmother lived with my grandparents, and her paternal grandmother lived next door to them. Her aunt and uncle lived next door to the paternal grandma, and the aunt's mother lived with them. When we all gathered for meals, we were almost at battalion strength. And I fed on the stories as much as the delicious, though thankfully not super healthy, food, the volume of which would have fed an actual battalion. My family loved to tell stories, and I soaked them in like a fine wine.

The best storyteller, hands-down, was my grandfather. He was … well, mischievous. He always had been. My favorite of his stories involved him and his brothers dropping a goat down the chimney of a neighbor's log cabin. My second favorite involved his picking up a live alligator by the jaws with the intent of transporting it in the trunk of our car from Hilton Head Island back to Greenville, S.C. where he intended to put it into the lake at Furman University and then report it to the Department of Natural Resources to see what would happen. I actually witnessed this one. The alligator tail-whipped my grandfather for the better part of a couple of minutes while he pondered a historic philosophical conundrum. Having picked up a live alligator, how do you turn it loose? That plan didn't pan out for him. Unfortunately, the time and space requirements for this Foreword won't accommodate those tales. This is David's book, after all. But you can just imagine.

I have to confess to being somewhat like my grandfather, though I have yet to pick up an alligator. I love to tell stories. Abraham Lincoln, a superior raconteur in his own right, once said that great storytellers never tell the stories for the benefit of the listener. My family would agree whole-heartedly. I have trotted out my threadbare yarns at dinner so many times that they now groan and roll their eyes before I even sit down at the table. It doesn't deter me. I launch right into, "Did I ever tell y'all about the time …."

My friend and colleague, David Flowers, has compiled in this book some wonderful anecdotes from his rather storied legal career. David is an exceptional attorney who has tried cases for civil plaintiffs and civil defendants and has taught trial advocacy at the law school at Wake Forest University and at other law schools. He tried and won a landmark sex-abuse case in which he obtained for his client a 100 million-dollar verdict. He is the only lawyer that I know who has done that.

But this isn't a self-indulgent "look-at-me" kind of book. The lawyers who would write such a book are the ones that subject all of us to the kind of derision embodied in the lawyer joke. These stories are funny, startling, poignant, and in some cases, all of the above. I am grateful to my friend for compiling these fine tales. I am honored that he would permit me to be a part of it.

I hope that as you read it, the book will give some insight as to why my son decided to become a lawyer, and why our profession is just the best one that there is, particularly where stories are concerned.

And I hope that after having read it, it will inspire you, when you gather with friends and family, not to be bashful about asking,

"Did I ever tell y'all about the time …."

Believe me, it'll be worth enduring the eye-rolling.

L. Lee Plumblee

INTRODUCTION

I didn't grow up wanting to be a lawyer. In my hometown of Goose Creek, South Carolina, college wasn't something that was mentioned much. Like all of my friends, I was just hoping to just get a good job out of high school. After brief stints as a janitor, truck driver, and warehouse worker, I was fortunate to get accepted into the apprenticeship program at Charleston Naval Shipyard, a federal civil service job. I applied for and got into Shop 56, the pipefitter shop. I had no idea what that entailed, but I knew it paid good money and was a shot at a well-paying career if I worked hard and stayed out of trouble. In the apprenticeship program, you not only learned a trade, you took college courses in subjects like mathematics, English, drafting, and metallurgy. I found that I really enjoyed the classroom, which was a new experience for me because I did not enjoy high school. That was due in part to a lack of being challenged, and the other part was for most of my high school years I was being sexually molested by a doctor at a hospital in downtown Charleston.

Inspired by the classroom work, while working at the

shipyard I started taking adult education classes in an accelerated evening degree program at what was then known as The Baptist College at Charleston. I discovered that I really enjoyed college and developed an insatiable desire to learn more and more.

During this time, I had numerous encounters with several coworkers at the shipyard who lamented what they would have done with their lives if they "had it to do over again". That recurring sentiment started really bothering me. I realized that I did not want to have a similar regret and knew that I was young enough that I still had a chance to change the trajectory of my life before I got too deep into the usual obligations and responsibilities that accrue in life.

I was married and my wife was pregnant with our first child. After a real estate deal went sour, my wife began developing difficulties with the pregnancy, caused by stress, so we had to bail on the deal. On the night we made that decision, I told her that I wanted to quit the shipyard (where she was also employed) and go to college and law school. I wanted to be a sports agent. I impressed upon her that the timing was perfect because I had two years of undergraduate work remaining and then three years of law school which meant I would be done with school and we could settle somewhere before our baby started school. That was important to us because we both were military brats who had moved a lot in our childhoods, and we wanted our children to have a more stable life. She cried most of the night. In the morning, she said "Let's do it." We immediately began making preparations to leave Charleston. Our first child, Louie, was born in November 1984.

The only school I wanted to attend was Clemson University. Fortunately, I was accepted and began classes in the summer of 1985. While attending Clemson, I worked at a nearby textile plant. It was a finishing plant where the woven fabrics were dyed and cut to order for apparel manufacturers. The job was perfect for me because I worked on what they called the mini-shift: 24 hours a week with full benefits. I began as a forklift operator and later transferred to the dye room.

I graduated from Clemson in May of 1987 and was accepted at Wake Forest University School of Law, where I began three months later. Wake Forest had a mandatory mock trial competition during the first semester, which I was compelled to participate in. It was lifechanging. During that competition, I realized that I was put on this earth to be a trial lawyer, not a sports agent. I then spent the remainder of my three years at Wake Forest finding and availing myself of every opportunity I could to be on my feet as an advocate. It was especially valuable because Wake Forest has an outstanding trial advocacy program, anchored for decades by Professor Carol Anderson, who is now a dear friend. Instead of focusing on grades as much as I should have, I sought opportunities to be on teams in both moot court and mock trial competitions. I was fortunate to be selected for several of these teams while I was there. Also, while in law school, I was lucky enough to get hired by two law firms that gave me unexpected opportunities. Both were plaintiff's firms, one a small-town general practice firm and the other a high end, complex litigation firm. I learned a lot from both and each in their own way began molding me into the lawyer that I became.

As graduation from law school loomed, I knew I wanted to do complex litigation from the plaintiff's side, including mass torts. I was recruited by a couple of defense firms, and even offered positions with them, but my heart really wanted to be on the other side.

And then along came John Hagins. I'll never forget our first meeting. It was raining cats and dogs and we both were soaked, sitting at that little café in Winston-Salem. Johnny had brought along the profit and loss statements for him and his partners to show me how much money they made. It was impressive, but I was looking for more than that. As Johnny started telling me about his practice, I was hooked. His practice consisted of complex plaintiff's work with a generous portion of insurance subrogation cases, related to fire losses, thrown in. Big and interesting stuff is all that he did. Bigger than life and interesting is all that Johnny was too. I accepted a position for a lot less than the other firms had offered.

I spent three years at Brown & Hagins and loved every minute of it. In addition to the plaintiff's work, Johnny reached out to the local State Farm Insurance Company claims office to get some insurance defense cases arising from minor automobile wrecks so I could get on my feet in courtrooms early and often to hone my trial skills before trying a case in which the stakes were considerably higher. That was an invaluable experience. I tried approximately 50 cases in my first couple of years, all over the Upstate, in front of a lot of judges and with a lot of lawyers.

After three years, the firm entered into negotiations with one of the largest firms in South Carolina, with the intent of merging. I was not interested in being in a big defense firm. Johnny wasn't either, so he started looking for alternatives. He began talking with Ness Motley Loadholt Richardson & Poole, a plaintiff's firm that made its name in asbestos litigation and litigated all over the United States. They were headquartered in Barnwell, SC with their main office in Charleston. They were one of the largest plaintiff's firms in the country and only handled large and complex litigation. It was a dream opportunity for me. The idea was that Johnny and I would open an office in Greenville for the firm. As our discussions got more serious, Johnny decided to go in a different direction. I called our contact at Ness Motley and asked who else they might be interested in heading up the Greenville office. I offered to approach whoever they mentioned. I really wanted to work for that firm. He told me they would just do it with me, which seemed utterly crazy to me: setting up a new office for THAT firm with only a third-year lawyer running it. Even though I was scared to death, I agreed to do it.

I spent three years at Ness Motley, and it was indeed a dream job. Due to the clout of the firm, I was able to litigate cases that I had dreamed of working on in law school. The one downside was the travel. My wife and I had twin daughters, Amy and Sarah, the month before I joined the firm (and we also bought a new house during that month for a true Stress Trifecta). Being away from home so much began to take a toll, so after three years, I knew my days at the firm were numbered when my daughter Sarah asked me on the phone one night to come stay at her house for a little while.

During those three years, I had acquired an interest in an unusual and dark corner of the law: representing victims of sexual abuse in civil litigation.

I've always had a keen intellectual interest in the First Amendment separation of church and state. I was aware that a certain church denomination routinely took the position that civil governments cannot tell them how to conduct their business, including the harboring, protection and moving around of pedophile priests. When I was hired by Ness Motley, I told my supervisor that I was interested in working on priest sexual abuse cases if the firm ever got any. Shortly after I was hired, we were asked to represent some victims of priest sexual abuse against the Diocese of Charleston. I was able to help those victims get a good result that could help them move forward with their lives. My name then got out into some victims' organizations across the country and the phone started ringing.

During that time, I made a call to a lawyer in Charleston who was also handling cases on behalf of victims of abuse. He liked filing lawsuits and trying to change the law for victims, especially with respect to the statute of limitations. It seemed like every new case I got, a defense lawyer would cite some new precedent that was not helpful for my clients, and it also seemed that every time I looked up the case, the plaintiff's lawyer was the same guy: Gregg Meyers.

I called Gregg and asked him to have lunch. He agreed.

Over lunch, I told him that he should stop filing the cases because the appellate courts in South Carolina were not sympathetic to victims and he was only making it harder every time he brought a new case and the courts rejected his arguments. He politely disagreed. However, at that lunch, we hit it off, even though we were complete opposites. He was erudite and urbane, juxtaposed to my jeans and baseball hat.

Shortly after that lunch, Gregg called me with an opportunity to work on a case together. He had been contacted by a Catholic priest who had been molested as a child by a Catholic priest. For twenty-five years, he had worked alongside his perpetrator in the same diocese and he finally just could not do it anymore. He hired us to present a claim and to extricate him from the diocese. It was a unique case because in addition to the usual molestation claim, it involved pension and employment issues. We were able to resolve the case, and in the process Gregg and I learned that our skill sets were unusually complementary. His strengths were my weaknesses and my strengths were his weaknesses. As he liked to tell people in the ensuing years, "Together, we make one pretty good lawyer."

In April 1997, shortly after resolving that case, I left Ness Motley and opened my own firm. Within weeks of that scary act, I got a call from Gregg about another case. A private school in Charleston had had a pedophile on their staff for ten years, and the senior administration officials knew during that entire time that this teacher was a pedophile. He molested several dozen boys at the school. When they were finally challenged by some parents to do something about this teacher, the administrators let him resign quietly and then recommended him for employment at other schools in the Charleston area, where he went on to molest many more students for another 15 years. That school was Porter-Gaud School and the Porter-Gaud litigation was, in some ways, the highwater mark of my legal career. It was also a curse that, in many ways, destroyed my life. After the verdict in December 2000, I needed to take some time off, so I began shutting down my practice.

That was my plan until Gregg got a call about a case that was uncannily identical to the Porter-Gaud case in a small town in North Carolina. Gregg persuaded me to stay on and help him with that case. At the conclusion of that case, about three years later, the reserves I had in my tank of emotions were completely depleted. I closed my practice for what I intended to be a one-year sabbatical. It turned out to be a three-year hiatus during which my marriage ended, I gave away all of my worldly possessions, and I wandered the western United States, spending weeks and months at a time in the woods.

In 2007, I tried to reenter the practice of law and was

persuaded by a friend to open a firm with him and two other lawyers. That did not last long. I had promised myself that, for my own wellbeing, I needed to avoid doing the abuse cases. As soon as word hit the street that I was practicing again, I started getting calls from lawyers with sexual abuse cases that they wanted to refer to me. I could only say "No" for so long. After a ridiculous disagreement with one of the partners in that firm, I left and hung my own shingle again. Like a moth to a flame, I got deeper into the abuse work than I had been before.

In the Summer and Fall of 2011, I became acutely suicidal and I was involuntarily committed to a mental hospital. While in the hospital, I placed myself on inactive status, in order to save myself from myself. I knew I could never practice law again.

After I got out of the hospital, I did a lot more wandering.

In 2014, while working at a remote campground in the Utah desert, I was asked to attend a dinner party in Hollywood related to a movie project based on the Porter-Gaud case. At that party, two men cornered me and asked me for permission to make a television series about my life and career. I sarcastically said, "Yeah, right." I tried to move past them, but they cut me off. They told me that they were already working on it and would like to discuss it with me. I excused myself, set my beer down on a table and got out of the party as fast as I could. I made a beeline for Joshua Tree National Park where I slept under the stars for a few nights. I called my friend who had arranged the dinner party, screenwriter Julie Lynch, and asked, "What the Hell?" She told me they were serious and that they had indeed already been working on a show. I asked what I needed to do. She said, "Just write. Write about your cases, write about your life, write about all of it, the highs and lows."

Shortly after that dinner party, unable to find any decent work, I decided to move to the island of Kauai. I had been doing volunteer work in the forests there for a number of years. Eradicating invasive plants and replanting native Hawaiian plants had become a passion of mine.

On my way to Kauai in September 2014, I was asked to again stop in Hollywood to be interviewed for a documentary film about the Porter-Gaud case, a different film than the one already mentioned.

I went to Kauai to hide and live the rest of my days, expecting human contact only with my children and employees at the local post office and grocery store. After buying a one-way ticket to the island, I was surprised (although I shouldn't have been) to discover that the organization that eradicated the invasive plants had no available jobs. The folly of what I had done became immediately apparent. Being in desperate straits, I decided that I would just live on the beach somewhere on the island until I could find a job.

Two things happened in the next few days that make it hard to argue against Divine Intervention. First, I found a job at a facility that needed someone to cut grass in exchange for accommodation in an immobile school bus. The lawn work paid for living in the bus, including all utilities and Wi-Fi. Second, I was able to get a job as a tour guide at a botanical garden. When I went for the interview, the interviewer, Nani, told me, "Look, I'm gonna hire you just because of your name, now tell me something about yourself."

So, while I lived in the school bus, I started writing about my career, in longhand, on legal pads. That exercise helped to turn my life around. Prior to that, I was in a very, very dark place and all I could remember from my career were the losses, the suicides… only the bad stuff. Once I started writing, I began to recall the funny cases, the crazy cases, and the good that I was able to do. Again, it was lifechanging. Much of that writing is included in this book.

Kauai saved my life. The job at the botanical garden, the garden itself, the people, and the culture collectively healed me in ways that were more profound and more expeditious than I could have ever imagined.

I returned to the mainland in December 2016.

My children started having children of their own, and I met someone who, in so many ways, I had been searching for for many years.

The documentary film about the Porter-Gaud litigation, *What Haunts Us,* is a powerful presentation that captures the emotional essence of that tragic story. It was nominated for an Emmy award in the category of Excellence in Documentary Filmmaking. When it was released in 2018, I was asked by the filmmaker, Paige Tolmach, to attend several film festivals across the country to answer questions about the story and discuss issues raised by the film. I agreed, and in attending those festivals, I was struck by the desire of many of the attendees for more information about the litigation. I was also really annoyed by the response of the current administration of Porter-Gaud School to Paige's film. Their dishonest reaction to the film persuaded me to polish off a manuscript about the case that I had begun many years before. I published that book, *Taming the Lion Tamers: The Inside Story of a Landmark Sex Abuse Case*, last year. It won third place in the True Crime category of a national book competition. The festival appearances and the publishing of that book helped me find my voice again.

Natali and I were married in December 2019. We live in an RV and plan on resuming the wandering, but in a very different way than I used to.

On a trip back to South Carolina from Kauai to see my kids, I was having lunch with a dear friend, Lee Plumblee. He told me about recently attending a funeral for his mentor. He said that it occurred to him during that funeral that the generation of lawyers before us was now dying off and with them, their stories were dying too. He said that we were next and that our generation needed to start writing our own stories before they were lost too. He paused for a long moment and then told me, "Of all the lawyers I know in our generation who need to write their stories down, you are the one who needs to write your stories." That conversation was the genesis of this book.

OPENING STATEMENT

One of the greatest, if not *the greatest*, storytellers in the history of the South Carolina Bar, Alex Sanders, has regaled generations of lawyers with his wisdom and wit. One thing that stuck with me from the many times I was privileged to hear his stories is that every time he was asked, "Is that true?", his steadfast reply was always, "Who cares if it's true, it's a great story!"

Trial lawyers do love to tell stories and any lawyer who has tried cases has their own collection to tell. All trial lawyers also love to pass along stories that they have heard from other lawyers. While these stories are generally intended to entertain, they can also be instructive or may even contain a kernel of something that may be planted and allowed to germinate and grow into an idea for a future trial… and hopefully be the genesis of yet *another* trial story. You'll see some examples of that in the Exhibits that I am about to present to you.

I had an unusual career. I think that is due to equal parts of taking unusual cases and handling them in unusual ways.

I hope you enjoy my stories.

EXHIBIT 1 - HAGINS

John A. Hagins, Jr. is a giant among South Carolina lawyers. Not because of his stature. He is short. He is well-known and universally liked. His letters are singularly entertaining. Many lawyers keep a file in their office of Johnny's letters. His antics in depositions and courtrooms are legendary. Almost every trial lawyer in South Carolina worth their salt has a Johnny Hagins story. I was privileged and honored to learn at the feet of this Master for the first three years of my career. Interestingly, I didn't learn much about the law from him. That's because he doesn't know much about the law. Instead, I learned many, many valuable life lessons from him, from what the judge really means when he/she says certain things to what all those forks and spoons and knives were doing surrounding my plate in fancy restaurants. I owe him more than I could ever repay for his patience and his guidance. Johnny is brilliant, witty, and a genuine joy to be around. I will forever be grateful to him for taking me under his wing and showing me the ropes, not only in the courtroom, but more importantly, outside of the courtroom.

The very first time I ever went to court with John Hagins was a case he had in the South Carolina Court of Appeals. He had gotten a substantial verdict in a case involving a golf course clubhouse that had burned to the ground. Johnny was able to demonstrate at trial that the club's golf cart charging system was defective and dangerous in that the carts could spontaneously ignite when they were charging overnight in the basement of the clubhouse.

The jury agreed that that was the cause of the fire and awarded Johnny's client more than a million dollars.

On appeal, the defendants argued, in part, that they were not liable and the jury's verdict should be overturned because of certain provisions of the Uniform Commercial Code. The specific provisions of the Uniform Commercial Code that were at issue not only escape me now (as does the rest of said Uniform Commercial Code), but the gist of them escaped me then. I knew it had something to do with the chain of commerce and particularly with the packaging and means of delivery of the golf carts to the country club from the manufacturer.

My predecessor at Brown & Hagins had written the brief for him. It focused on the pertinent provisions of the UCC. The associate later left the firm and I was hired to replace her.

It was just coincidental that Johnny was doing the oral

argument in the case on one of my first days at the firm, so he took me along to observe. It was my first dose of what I refer to as "The Hagins Shuffle".

Johnny is a brilliant lawyer, but he comes across to people who don't know him as kind of a bumbling goof. He reminded me, and others, of the television character Columbo. When we got to the Court of Appeals, I learned that all three judges on the panel were personal friends of Johnny, including one who was his roommate in law school.

As Johnny launched into his argument, he began discussing one of the provisions of the Uniform Commercial Code at issue in the case.

He was on a roll and it seemed he was carrying the day when one of the judges interrupted him and asked, "Mr. Hagins, isn't your argument contradicted by the Reporter's Comments to that section?" (The Reporter's Comments are explanatory material in the Uniform Commercial Code to help make the thick statutory language more understandable. They are an integral part of the Uniform Commercial Code.)

After an awkward pause, Johnny's response was, "The what, Your Honor?"

I noticed some worried looks in the courtroom.

The judge said, "The Reporter's Comments, Mr. Hagins." The judge then read from the Reporter's Comments related to the particular section Johnny was arguing about. It was clear to everyone in the courtroom that the Reporter's Comments did indeed completely contradict the argument that Johnny was making to the court.

Johnny paused, grasped the podium with both hands, looked down at his shoes, stood there for a couple of very uncomfortable moments, and then looked up and said, "Your Honors, I am just a simple sex and violence lawyer, I don't know anything about the Uniform Commercial Code."

The courtroom erupted in laughter, including all three judges.

As the laughter began to ebb, Johnny tried to regain his footing. Just as he resumed his argument on a different point, a different judge interrupted him and said, "Hold on Mr. Hagins. I'm curious, if you only handle *simple* sex and violence cases, what do you do with the complex ones that come into your office?"

The courtroom erupted again.

For the rest of the argument, the discussion centered around the sex and violence cases that Hagins had in his office at that time and ones that might come his way in the future.

When his time expired, Johnny entertained the judges for a few more minutes and then took his seat.

In spite of his dalliance with the Uniform Commercial Code, Johnny's verdict was upheld because the associate had written a solid brief. It was only the first example of many that I witnessed over several years where Johnny *appeared* to not know what he was doing, but he won in the end.

Another example of The Hagins Shuffle occurred when Johnny and his co-counsel were aligned with some out-of-state lawyers in a pretty significant business litigation case. The out-of-state lawyers were interested in working together and suggested that if

Johnny would share with them his trial strategy, they would share with him some documents and their own strategy. Johnny agreed and within a few days he received a letter detailing the lawyers' strategy and enclosing some documents. Johnny was grateful and demonstrated his gratitude by immediately writing back to these lawyers and disclosing his trial strategy: He told them that he and his co-counsel, Doug Patrick, planned to wear their lucky ties to the trial!

Another letter that Johnny wrote was one of my favorites. He and his wife Priscilla had been at a dinner party the night before. When they got home, his wife told him it appeared that he liked a certain lawyer who was also at the dinner party. The first thing he did when he came into the office the next morning was to write a letter to this lawyer in which he said, "When we arrived home last night my wife informed me that it appeared that I may like you. This letter is to set the record straight. I have never liked you. I do not like you now. And I have no intention of liking you in the future. Sincerely, John Hagins"

Johnny came into my office one morning and asked what I was doing. As I started to tell him, he cut me off and told me to stop whatever it was because he had something he needed me to work on immediately. He went back into his office across the hall and returned with an empty potato chip bag.

He told me he had been eating the chips the night before, while watching television. During a commercial break, he noticed a sticker on the bag that said, "Manager's Special $1.79". To satisfy his insatiable curiosity, he peeled back the sticker to see how much money Priscilla had saved by buying the "Manager's Special". He was shocked to see that the regular price of the chips was $1.49. He became irate that the "Manager's Special" was to increase the price of the chips by 20%.

He believed it was false advertising and wanted to file a lawsuit on behalf of everyone who had bought the same "Manager's Special". He instructed me to immediately begin drafting a class-action complaint.

I spent most of the day working on it, until one of the other partners came into my office in the afternoon and asked what I was doing. When I excitedly told him about the class action lawsuit that we were going to file, he ordered me to stop immediately.

He went into Johnny's office and had a very animated conversation, which is how most conversations with John Hagins were conducted. Johnny was adamant that we were going to file this class-action lawsuit. The other partner was adamant that we were not. He left Johnny's office to go get some of the other partners to come and collectively persuade Johnny to knock it off.

In the end, Johnny relented, and I never got to file the Potato Chip Manager's Special False Advertising Class-Action lawsuit.

:-(

Johnny was involved in a complex business litigation case involving three men who all used to be friends and who were previously in business together, creating medical products out of foam rubber. Some of these products were as simple as a triangular piece of foam that kept a patient from rolling over on their back to more complex products, all made from foam rubber.

When these three friends went their separate ways, they all stayed in the foam rubber medical products business, and spent the next several years suing each other, alleging that each of them was stealing the others' ideas, products, and customers. While there *may* have been some merit to some of their allegations, the true value of the case was the entertaining way in which John Hagins handled the representation of his client.

Many of the products that these gentlemen developed closely resembled products that one or more of the others had already developed. One of the issues in the cases was how close the products could be to each other and still receive a patent, or not infringe one of the others' patents. Johnny became exasperated at how a slight nuance would embolden his client or one of the other men to think they had a new product.

So, during a deposition in which Johnny was deposing one of the other litigants, he brought along a big piece of foam rubber. At a point in the deposition where he was asking about how much research and development generally went into the different iterations of these products, the deponent got very defensive about Johnny's sarcasm and his mocking tone.

There was some increasingly heated back and forth, when suddenly Johnny put the big hunk of foam rubber on the table and reached into his briefcase. He brought out a very large knife, actually a huge knife, and started wildly slicing the foam rubber in various ways. Every time he sliced a random piece off of the hunk, he would ask the deponent if he could patent the slice and/or the remaining hunk. He did that over and over again.

It was wildly entertaining. I think some of the people in the room were scared, but Johnny was absolutely serious about the point he was making.

On our way back to the office, I asked Johnny if he wanted me to file patent applications for his new medical products.

EXHIBIT 2 – GREGG MEYERS

The opposite of my doppelganger on this earth is Gregg Meyers. He is erudite and very urbane. I am very blue collar and always wore jeans and a ballcap to the office and depositions. The only thing I ever found that we had in common was a shared desire to go after anyone who hurt a child. We worked together on cases for almost 15 years, but we approached them and handled them in very different ways. He loves legal research; I would rather take a beating. He plays the long game, hoping to persuade appellate courts to change the law; I prefer to bash wrongdoers' heads in, in the moment. He is professional and deferential in depositions and courtrooms; I am… not those things in depositions and courtrooms. As mentioned in the Introduction, we discovered that our very different approaches and demeanors collectively made us one pretty good lawyer. Interestingly, we rarely disagreed about our strategic approach to sex abuse cases. I was privileged and honored to have been beside him in the trenches for so many years. He is the embodiment of a courageous and brilliant lawyer. He represents what the practice of law should be: a noble endeavor to help those who need a champion.

Gregg is much more educated, polished, and refined than I

am. He is very well-schooled in the classics and in history.

In a deposition in which neither one of us were actively participating, he wrote something on a Post-it note and handed it to me. It said, "This guy is Johnson's Boswell".

I wrote on the note, "This is obviously a literary reference. You forget that I went to Goose Creek High School. I have no idea what you're talking about. Fuck you." I handed it back to him.

Another instance of the refinement disparity between Gregg and me occurred in the home of a couple who were witnesses in a case we were working on. They were both in wheelchairs with their left legs in casts. They had been riding on a tandem bicycle and got hit by car.

They let us in the front door and as we were walking, and rolling, down the hallway, Gregg and I noticed two dogs, both greyhounds. Gregg commented on the greyhounds and told a brief story about Odysseus and his greyhounds.

Gregg turned to me and said, "What were the names of

Odysseus's dogs?"

I walked up close behind him and whispered, "Fuck you".

Gregg is a gadget geek. He likes cutting-edge technology and always likes to have the latest thing.

Way back when, a Palm Pilot was cutting-edge, and it's funny to remember, but it was really cool that it took pictures.

Gregg and I were deposing an adverse witness who we were pretty sure was going to lie. During the entire deposition, while I was focused on the witness and my questions, Gregg was constantly taking photographs of the guy surreptitiously and showing them to me.

It seems so blasé now, but at the time it really was pretty cool.

Gregg handled a lot of *qui tam* cases, also known as False Claims Act cases. They arise from a federal statute that permits any citizen who has knowledge of a fraud being perpetrated on the federal government to file a lawsuit to recover the fraudulently obtained funds.

One of those cases he handled was against one of the largest construction companies in the world, which was headquartered in Greenville. Two whistleblowers had brought suit against the construction company for repairs done to navy housing and the naval base in Charleston after damage from Hurricane Hugo in 1989.

The defense lawyer was from Greenville. He was generally liked, but was known to be quite arrogant, and supremely confident in his legal abilities. He was also known to play games in discovery including, in that case, producing 13 *rooms* of boxes of documents, and reshuffling the documents, including moving them from room to room, at the end of the day while Gregg was sifting through them. Gregg eventually sought and got a court order halting that ridiculous shenanigan.

In spite of that nonsense, Gregg went out of his way, as he always did with defense lawyers (much to my chagrin!), to be cordial to this particular lawyer. He calculated that it would cause the opposing counsel to underestimate him.

On the first day of a three week trial in Charleston, while waiting for the jury to enter the courtroom, this defense lawyer stepped over to Gregg's table and, standing over him, whispered, "Well, one of us is about to learn something." Gregg did not respond, but inwardly agreed that the guy was probably right.

After the jury returned a $3 million verdict for Gregg's client, the jury foreman told the local newspaper, "It seemed like a simple case to us."

One of the differences between Gregg and me is that he never asked that defense lawyer what he learned, but I would've asked that guy every single opportunity I had for years thereafter what he had learned. In fact, every time I saw the guy after that verdict, I was tempted to ask him what he had learned from Gregg.

One of the best examples of how Gregg's brain and mine worked very differently occurred in a courtroom in Greenville. We were there to begin the trial of a case involving a young girl who had been molested by a teacher. One of our unconventional tactics was to bring suit on behalf of the parents for the harm done to their relationship with their child, essentially a loss of consortium claim. (Most people are not aware that the verdict in the Porter-Gaud case was awarded to the father of a victim, not a victim.) We did this to try to minimize the child's role in the litigation, knowing there would be plenty of time to file the child's case after they reach the age of majority.

Brown Parkinson was defending the case and he had been requesting a continuance, which we were not in a position to agree to. At the trial, he tried again to get a delay from Judge Choppy Patterson. Judge Patterson was not going to grant it, so Brown made a Rule 12 Motion to Dismiss the case, arguing that parents did not have a cognizable claim in South Carolina for harm done to their child. It was a motion that Gregg and I had faced, and fended off, many times before. However, this time was different. Judge Patterson indicated that he was inclined to grant the motion.

Immediately, Gregg's mind and mine went down separate paths. He was thinking about an appeal, so he was careful to make sure he had everything in the record that he would need to argue the appeal. When he was finished addressing the judge, I stood and made a Motion to Substitute Parties, arguing that we could just substitute the young girl in as the plaintiff and that we were ready to try her case because the liability proof was going to be identical. I argued that the only difference in the trial would be damages and since the South Carolina Supreme Court had previously held that molestation of a child is inherently injurious, we could just let the jury decide on damages.

Judge Patterson seemed to like that idea. He asked Brown what he thought. Brown resisted, saying he was not prepared to try that case. There was some back and forth, with the judge increasingly warming to the idea of substituting the parties and going ahead with a trial that morning.

In the end, Judge Patterson granted the motion to substitute, but gave Brown 30 days to prepare for that trial.

Afterwards, Gregg and I were both struck by how differently we had approached that moment, with him thinking about the long game and me staying in the moment.

A lawyer from an out-of-state firm became involved in a case after it had already been proceeding for a considerable amount of time. In a hearing, she was trying to recount for the judge the facts and history of the case up to that point, of which she had no real understanding. She kept either ignorantly making inaccurate statements or was intentionally misrepresenting the facts.

After she had done it a few times, Gregg stood up and objected and said, "That's not true, Your Honor."

The lawyer tried to recast what she was saying and made it even worse.

Gregg stood again and said, "That's not true, Your Honor."

Over the next several minutes, as the lawyer was trying to give her version of what she thought happened, Gregg kept bouncing up and telling the judge, "That's not true, Your Honor".

Finally, she had had enough, and she said rather loudly as Gregg stood to object again, "Would you stop interrupting me?"

To which Gregg replied, "When you stop lying, I'll stop interrupting."

In the Porter-Gaud litigation, we were arguing that the administrators who favorably recommended a serial pedophile to other schools should be held legally responsible for every child who was molested at any school to which they had recommended the perpetrator, because they knew he was a serial pedophile. In the law, it is known as a duty.

As Gregg was arguing that the court should find them responsible for the molestation of all "downstream" victims, the judge asked if Gregg had a case or a precedent for such a broad interpretation of 'duty'.

Gregg paused for what became a rather awkward moment and then said, "Your honor, I don't have a case because I am happy to report to the court that in the history of Anglo-American jurisprudence, no school has ever acted as badly as this one, so there is no precedent."

Gregg did most of our legal arguments. In one particular argument, he and Circuit Court Judge Daniel Pieper were discussing some esoteric legal nicety that I frankly did not understand, but they both seemed to be enjoying themselves.

Judge Pieper was an intellectual and really enjoyed legal discourse with a lawyer who enjoyed it as much as he did.

It seemed clear to me that Gregg was carrying the day and we were going to win the argument, so toward the end of it, while Gregg was speaking, I tugged on the hem of his suit coat, which was usually a sign that I wanted to alert him to something or suggest something for him to say.

He asked the judge if he could have a moment. He then leaned down towards me so I could have his ear.

I whispered in his ear, "I'm falling in love with you right now."

It was the only time in our years of work together that I remember seeing Gregg get flustered. He had to ask the judge for another moment so he could collect his thoughts.

At the next break, he rather sternly told me, "Don't ever do that to me again".

One of the things I loved about doing plaintiff's work was that you never really knew what was going to walk in the door. The craziest example that I know of happened to Gregg.

He was in his office one day just working at his desk when a former client walked in with one of those little igloo coolers that you take your lunch to work in, where the lid rolls over to the side. Gregg knew the guy fairly well, so he just said, "What have you got?"

The man opened the cooler to reveal a human skeleton.

Gregg was aghast. He made it clear he did not want the skeleton in his office, but the guy insisted on telling why he was there and why he was toting around a human skeleton.

This gentleman told Gregg that he and his wife had purchased a piece of land outside of Charleston, on which they planned to build their dream home. They hired a contractor and after some length of time they moved into the house.

After moving in, the gentleman started noticing depressions in the yard in various places. He wondered what they were. He decided to dig in one of the depressions and that's where he found the skeleton. He did some research and discovered that the piece of land they had purchased was an old graveyard that had been used for a couple hundred years.

The contractor had merely bulldozed the land and pushed most of the graves to the side to build the house.

Gregg was interested in the case. He decided to file a lawsuit and had the skeleton in his office for a few days until he realized it was actually a crime to mess with a dead body.

He called the client to come and get the skeleton out of his office.

Gregg and I were involved in a case in which he did most of the work and had all the contact with the clients. In fact, until we got to a mediation conference, I had never even met the clients. As Gregg was preparing them for the mediation, they asked him why I was coming if I had not worked on the case. Gregg told them that he couldn't explain why, but he promised there would be a reason that they would want me at the mediation.

The case was very contentious. One of our clients was in a dispute with her three siblings about the disposition of some jointly owned property. The client was afraid that her siblings would do something nefarious, like agreeing to sell the property at a fire sale price and then reacquire the property, essentially cutting her out of her lawful interest.

During the mediation conference, it appeared that we were not going to be able to settle the case because the siblings could not agree on a price at which to list the property, or on a fair way to collectively decide whether to sell or not. Our client was always going to be outvoted three to one.

When it appeared we were at a dead end and the mediator, Barron Grier, was ready to declare an impasse and end the mediation, I was sitting at the far end of a very long conference table, a good distance from Gregg, the clients and Barron. I asked them to give me a few more minutes.

I was putting the final touches on a proposal that I had come up with and I wanted to finish it before I showed it to them. So, they chatted for a few minutes.

When I concluded my work, I got their attention and told them about my idea. In a general sense, I proposed to sell the property for an agreed upon amount, high enough to satisfy all of the siblings. If it sold for that amount, the siblings would all get an equal share of the proceeds. However, if it sold for less than that amount, a sliding scale would kick in whereby the lower the price, the less of a share for the other three siblings and a higher share for our client. So, if the siblings wanted to get the property at a fire sale, our client would get the lion's share of the proceeds of the sale. I showed them the numbers I had worked up.

After an awkward silence, Barron said, "David, that's brilliant!"

As soon as those words left his mouth, Gregg looked at the

clients and very loudly said, "I told you!!"

The case was settled.

In the Porter-Gaud litigation, one of the things that is not widely known is that it was a series of trials. The first settled after three days of trial. The second ended in a mistrial at the end of the plaintiffs' case. As a result, Gregg and I were able to speak to several jurors from those two trials to see what they thought about our case and our presentation. It was invaluable.

One of the many things we learned was that, even before the close of evidence, both juries were preparing to award very substantial damages. When I say substantial, I mean way more than we were even planning on suggesting to them.

In one conversation with some of the jurors from the first trial, Gregg asked the jurors, "We were thinking about asking for about $10 million in damages. What do you think of that?" Every single one of them said it was not enough. One said she was thinking about $50 million. Another said, "Millions? Honey, I was thinking about billions!" The woman beside her said, "Me too."

After the second trial, the judge indicated to us that he was going to bifurcate the trial, splitting it into two distinct phases: an actual damages phase and, if the plaintiff prevailed in that phase, a punitive damage phase. That got me to thinking about punitive damages more than we had considered up to that point.

South Carolina law prevented the jury from awarding punitive damages against the school. However, if we were able to prove gross negligence against the individual defendants, we could seek punitive damages from the two administrators who had so badly created the horror that harmed so many kids. The biggest problem for us in that regard was that by the time of the trials, both of those men were dead, one by natural causes and one committed suicide right before we took his deposition.

While mulling over the judge's decision about bifurcation, I got an idea about how to present a punitive damages argument to the jury. I was driving home from Charleston to Greenville, so I had plenty of time to think about it. An argument began to come together in my head. I called Gregg. I got his voicemail, so I left him this message: "I know this is going to sound really, really, really crazy, but if you get us to the jury, I'm going to get $100 million in punitive damages."

He spent that entire weekend needling me about it, and justifiably so. I knew it was bold, but I really thought my idea might work. In the trial, the plaintiff prevailed in the initial phase, with the jury awarding the plaintiff $15 million in actual damages, so we proceeded to a punitive phase.

At the end of the evidence in the punitive phase, I gave the closing argument that I had put together on the drive home. The jury found for the plaintiff again and awarded $45 million in punitive damages against each of the dead men's estates, for a total of $90 million in punitive damages.

As the jury was being polled to confirm that this was the verdict of all of them, Gregg leaned over to me and whispered, in mock seriousness, "You said $100 million. You keep screwing this up and I'm not going to let you do the closing argument anymore."[1]

[1] I was deeply honored when The Honorable Joseph F. Anderson chose to include this argument in its entirety in his seminal book on closing arguments, *The Lost Art: An Advocate's Guide to Closing Arguments*. You can also find this argument in my previous book about the Porter- Gaud litigation, *Taming the*

There were only two times that I recall, in all of our years working together, that I declined to get involved in a case which Gregg then decided to handle on his own.

The first case was against a very well-known hip-hop singer. There was a particular moment in a videotape, which was the main piece of evidence supporting the plaintiff's claim, that I thought would be fatal to any attempt to persuade the jury to believe the plaintiff's story. I told him I thought the case could not be won and wished him luck. He ended up getting a $20 million default judgment.

The second case was a defamation case on behalf of a medical doctor. There were some aspects of the case that I was troubled by so, again, I declined. In this case, I suggested to Gregg an idea for a closing argument, which he then used to obtain a $30 million judgment!

EXHIBIT 3 – LAW SCHOOL

During law school, I had to work fulltime all three years. I was fortunate to find jobs with two law firms that helped mold me into the lawyer that I became. In my first year, I clerked for a firm in Kernersville, NC, Wolfe & Collins. They had a general practice and it exposed me to a wide range of legal matters. During my second and third years of law school I clerked for a plaintiff's personal injury firm in Winston-Salem, NC, Lewis & Daggett. It was there that I discovered and nurtured my passion for representing plaintiffs in civil litigation. Mike Lewis is a lawyer's lawyer. He taught me a great deal about the practice of law and even let me get on my feet in real courtrooms, handling real cases pursuant to the North Carolina court rule that allowed third year students to appear in court with a sponsoring attorney.

The Town of Kernersville had its own set of local laws, just like every other small municipality in America. While I was working at Wolfe & Collins, John Wolfe was the town attorney (and he still is!). The town wanted a new ordinance for either excessive dog barking or a leash law, I can't recall which. In the context of drafting that, the town council decided to update its entire Code of

Ordinances. John let me take the lead on finding and suggesting proposed ordinances on a number of issues, as well as updating the existing ones. We were able to present to the council a proposed wholly revamped Code of Ordinances, which they enacted.

John's partner, Buddy Collins, was mostly a criminal defense lawyer. He had an interesting practice, partially because whenever he was having a slow day, he would head to the courthouse in Winston-Salem or Greensboro on criminal court days and hang out in the hallways, making himself available to anyone who needed a lawyer but had not yet bothered to procure one. It was a very lucrative exercise.

Buddy had several interesting cases. Among my favorites was a case in which his client was accused of speeding. On the citation, the police officer had left blank the box in which the speed of the accused was to be recorded.

At the trial, the officer testified that the accused was exceeding the speed limit but did not specify a speed. One of the cardinal rules in trial law is never ask a question while doing cross-examination that you don't already know the answer to.

When it was Buddy's turn to cross examine the police officer, he could not help himself. He asked the officer how fast his client was going.

The officer replied, "I don't know."

Instead of sitting down and then moving to dismiss the case, Buddy asked the following question, "Well if you don't know how fast he was going, how could you write him a citation for speeding?"

The officer obliged, "Well, that day, I was doing radar duty, and as a car was proceeding around a bend toward me, I locked in their speed at 77 miles per hour. Just as I turned on my lights to pursue them, your client passed that car."

Buddy then sheepishly said, "No more questions, Your Honor."

His client was convicted of speeding.

My first experience in court with John Wolfe was a memorable one. He was representing a minor defendant in a huge criminal case in federal court in Greensboro which involved a car theft ring in Greensboro that would steal certain cars in central North Carolina and then ship them to New York City where they would be sold to buyers who had no idea the cars had been stolen. The defendants in NYC would actually place an order for a specific year, model, and color and then their codefendants in North Carolina would find that exact car and steal it. I'll never forget that one of the main defendants looked just like Santa Claus.

There was a very dramatic moment in the trial when the prosecutor asked a cooperating witness whether he recognized one of the main defendants in the courtroom. The witness replied in the affirmative. The prosecutor then asked the witness to point out that person for the jury, a common moment in a lot of criminal trials. However, this time it was different than most. The witness pointed to one of the defense lawyers in the case. The prosecutor was as surprised as everyone else. The prosecutor pressed the witness to be sure, but the witness could not be moved. When the witness indicated that he was absolutely certain that the person that he was pointing out was one of the co-conspirators, the federal judge called for a break. After the jury left the courtroom, the judge indicated that either the witness was mistaken, or a certain lawyer may want to be looking for his own lawyer.

John had a case in which his client had received a ticket after attending a NASCAR case at Rockingham. The guy's girlfriend was with him at the time, so she was going to testify as a witness. When we arrived for the trial, our client was dressed in khakis and a dress shirt, in accordance with John's instructions. However, his girlfriend was a different story. She was dressed in what could only be described as a risqué prom dress. And, not to put too fine of a point on it, she was overflowing the dress. It was, frankly, distracting.

When she was on the stand testifying, the judge was mesmerized. When her testimony was finished, the judge, a friend of John's, summoned counsel to the bench.

During what is known as a bench conference, the judge told John, "If you ever do that to me again, I am going to hold YOU in contempt of court".

John said he had nothing to do with it, but the judge didn't believe him.

The first big case I worked on with John and Buddy was a "spot zoning" case. The generally accepted definition of spot zoning is "the process of singling out a small parcel of land for a use totally different from that of the surrounding area, for the benefit of the owner of such property and to the detriment of other owners." We represented a property owner who had land that was adjacent to a parcel in which the neighbor wanted to open a bar in an abandoned gas station. My initial impression was that I could not possibly imagine anything more boring than zoning. I wanted to work on exciting and interesting stuff. I could not have been more wrong.

The case ended up going to the North Carolina Supreme Court. I had to do a lot of legal research (which I HATE) and John and Buddy gave me a long leash with which to craft arguments and briefs. I became very fascinated by spot zoning. I ended up being very excited about the case and what I learned was that you can't judge a legal case by its cover.

Probably the most interesting case I worked on during my tenure at Wolfe & Collins involved a mother and adult son who lived together in a house within the town limits. They did not take care of their house or yard. Their residence was the source of many complaints to the town about garbage, rats, and other problems. The town started issuing warnings to the residents to clean up their property. The town never got a response. Finally, in frustration, the town notified the mother and son that if they did not clean up their property by a specific date, the town was going to clean it up for them and then charge them for the expense. The town even dropped off a dumpster in front of the house to indicate how serious they were.

On the morning of the deadline, the mother and son got up and got ready for work. When they were ready, the mother went out and got in the car. The son then walked through the house, pouring gasoline throughout the house. When he reached the front door, he ignited it. The explosion blew him almost to the street. He was severely injured, including serious burns. The house mostly burned down. The man was hospitalized for quite a while. He was charged with arson. During the cleanup of the remains of the house, a huge mound of coins was discovered in one room. It was several feet high and would've taken up most of the room. I was tasked with developing a legal argument by which the town could seize that money to repay them for the fire department's expenses incurred in fighting the fire.

One of the strangest moments I ever witnessed in a courtroom happened in a case when I was working with Mike Lewis. He was trying a run-of-the-mill wreck case. He represented a young man in his late teens or early twenties. When the young man was on the stand being cross-examined by the defense lawyer, the lawyer started asking him about being in a juvenile detention program when he was a young teen. Mike objected, but the judge let the lawyer continue the line of questioning. The young man had been kicked out of that program. When the lawyer told the young man to tell the jury why he was kicked out of the program, Mike objected again and argued that it wasn't relevant.

The judge summoned counsel to the bench, where the defense lawyer said, "Judge, you're going to want to hear this." Mike wanted to know what was going on. The defense lawyer would not disclose what he knew, but he made a sufficient argument on relevancy, and the judge let him continue. He asked the young man again why he was kicked out of the program. The plaintiff responded that he had done something wrong.

When he was pressed on what he had done, he refused to answer, so the lawyer said, "Isn't it true that you were kicked out of the program because you got caught having sex with a chicken?" It created one of the weirdest silences that I've ever heard in a courtroom.

The client admitted that it was true.

The jury awarded him nothing.

However, that revelation seemed to rock Mike Lewis' world. For weeks, if we were driving in the car, or he just had a quiet moment, he would say softly to himself, "Sex with a chicken?"

A few of the most valuable lessons I learned while clerking for Mike Lewis were unexpected and were in an inverse manner. I learned them from Mike's partner, and the lessons were like when you learn what not to do by watching an older sibling get in trouble. There were three such lessons that occurred in two separate trials. The first was a dental malpractice case that was pending in federal court and was tried by Mike's partner. I think it was his first professional malpractice trial. It was a serious case and believed by Mike and his partner to be one that should result in a substantial verdict.

At the trial, handled entirely by Mike's partner, there was a stunning development at the end of the plaintiff's case. The plaintiff had done a good job with his testimony and the plaintiff's evidence concluded right before lunch with the plaintiff's expert witness. During the lunch break, Mike's partner was slapping high fives with the client and boasting about how well the case was going. I suspect he was even beginning to spend his fee in his head.

When we returned from lunch, the defense made a motion for a directed verdict (dismissal) on the grounds that the plaintiff's expert witness never testified that the defendant dentist's care was below the standard of care. In any professional malpractice case, the plaintiff has to present evidence that the care provided by the professional was less than a normal professional would provide.

The judge granted the motion and, in his ruling, stated that he himself noticed that the plaintiff rested without ever asking that critical question. The plaintiff was devastated. Mike's partner was beside himself. When we got back to the office, Mike pulled me aside to ask me lots of questions about what happened. He told me that the judge had called him before we returned to the office and told Mike that he did not want the partner back in his courtroom.

The other two lessons came in a very sad case in which a young woman was killed in a really bad car wreck. She had been recently married and her husband was understandably devastated. In preparing for the trial, Mike's partner learned that there was a certain photograph of the young couple that was particularly difficult for the husband to look at without breaking down and sobbing. Mike's partner decided to work that into his trial strategy. Unfortunately, the execution of that strategy missed the mark.

Usually, with a piece of evidence like that, you would ease into it and maybe build to a dramatic moment. Instead, Mike's partner pulled it out very dramatically and showed it to the husband when it was apropos of nothing at that moment. The husband immediately burst into tears, and it came across as contrived. I thought (even as a law student) that it was a huge mistake.

The final mistake was even worse. The plaintiff offered an expert witness to testify about the economic loss to the husband, a subject that causes some to wince in such a case, but it is an appropriate part of any wrongful death case. The expert had created a particular document that Mike's partner had blown up which summarized the different categories of damages. As I recall, three columns, A, B, and C, when added together equaled Column D, which was the total of each horizontal line, and then in the bottom right corner was a figure that represented the total economic loss according to the expert. I thought the expert did a good job explaining the information on the chart.

When it was time for the defense lawyer to cross-examine, he got the expert to explain again that A+B+C=D. Then the lawyer pulled out a pocket calculator. He slowly (and dramatically) punched in the numbers from the first three columns and his result was different than what was on the chart. It was humiliating for the expert as the lawyer went through every line on the chart and showed how it was all wrong. When the expert tried to explain how he may have erred with the math, he only made it worse. When Mike's partner tried to rehabilitate the expert on redirect, he only made it worser.

EXHIBIT 4 – INSURANCE DEFENSE

Trying a case from the defense perspective is very different than trying the same case from the plaintiff's perspective. The plaintiff must put forth evidence to prove a case. The defense only has to shoot holes in the plaintiff's case. In my first two years, I tried a number of cases from the defense side that involved car wrecks with very minimal or, in some cases, no damage to either vehicle. It was invaluable, and often quite fun…

A woman was sitting in line in traffic on Whitehorse Road in Greenville early one morning, waiting to turn into a Hardee's restaurant to get breakfast, when her vehicle was struck in the rear by another driver. She indicated to the emergency responders that she was hurt. They took her to the hospital. Among other tests, they took some X-rays. A couple of weeks later, she discovered that she was pregnant, and had been pregnant at the time of the accident and X-rays. She became very distressed about the possibility that the X-rays may cause her child to be born with birth defects.

After the child was born, the woman filed a lawsuit and alleged that her newborn son did indeed have a birth defect: he had an extremely small penis. The lawsuit was not brought on behalf of her child. It was filed by her to recover damages for the emotional distress she alleged she was going to suffer for the rest of her life because her son had an extremely small penis.

A man was on his way to work in the predawn hours, driving a Volkswagen Beetle. Suddenly out of the dark, a horse appeared, standing across his lane. The Beetle struck the horse in the stomach, forcing the bulk of the animal into the windshield, smashing it and injuring the man pretty severely. He was knocked unconscious. The Beetle's forward momentum sent it off the road, through a ditch, across a small field, carrying the horse the whole way, and into a John Deere dealership that contained mostly lawn and residential equipment, not commercial tractors.

The horse was also severely injured and apparently was also rendered unconscious for a period of time. When the horse came to, it was frightened and tried to get out of the dealership, which was very unfamiliar to it. The horse then spent some time completely trashing the entire showroom of the dealership. The litigation ended up being much more complex than one would think because not only did the man sue the owner of the horse, but the John Deere dealership also sued the farmer and the man who struck the horse.

An insurance company hired me to represent a young man who had been accused of leaving a car in the traffic lanes of a highway… on a curve… on a dark road… at night. Another driver came around the curve and crashed into the back of the abandoned car. The driver sustained some injuries, so they sued the owner of the abandoned car. It took some time to track this young man down. I finally found that he worked at a metal scrap yard in Greenville. I went to see him one day and found him on a large crane with an electromagnet at the end of a long boom and wire. He was picking up huge piles of metal and moving them from one spot in the scrap yard to another. I tried to get his attention. He wouldn't look at me. I can only imagine how strange it was for him to see a stranger in a suit standing in the middle of the scrap yard waving his arms. I hollered to him that I'd been hired to represent his interests in a lawsuit. He just kept ignoring me. So, I raised my voice louder and said, "Either you talk to me now or I'll go get a deputy sheriff and have you escorted to my office." That got his attention.

He turned off the crane and climbed down to speak to me. I learned he was on parole, so he wanted no part of deputy sheriffs. When I explained to him why I was there, he explained that the reason he left the car in the middle of the road was that when it broke down he was going to get help, but he couldn't push it off the road by himself. When he came back and saw the accident, he realized he might be in some trouble, and being on parole, he just ran.

When the opposing lawyer later took his deposition, he asked the young man how he could afford to just leave a car in the middle of the road and not come back to get it. The young man replied, "I had just bought it that afternoon for $25 and a six-pack of beer."

One of my earliest cases was an interesting and needlessly complex case. It was an automobile accident case that involved, as I recall, nine cars. It was a chain reaction wreck. There was only one serious injury: one of the drivers had a broken leg. All of the other drivers and passengers had varying degrees of soft tissue injuries.

What made it so complex was most of the drivers filed a lawsuit which required the insurance companies for each car to hire a defense lawyer, which would have been in addition to all of the plaintiffs' lawyers that were already engaged. I don't remember the precise number of lawyers, but it exceeded the number of claimants which was about 14.

When we were called for a status conference to work out the logistics of a trial, the judge, Choppy Patterson, was not interested in trying the case. He put some pretty harsh restrictions on the lawyers' ability to conduct the trial. For example, he limited opening statements to five minutes *per car*. He limited the questioning of witnesses and closing arguments in a similar fashion. We all knew the trial would be a logistical nightmare. So, Judge Patterson ordered us to get together and see if we could get it settled.

Somehow, we all found a day on our calendars before the scheduled trial. I suggested to the other defense lawyers that we talk to our respective insurance companies and tell them, "Look, give me some money that I can throw in a pot." All of the defense lawyers got some money to throw into this "pot" and then we invited the plaintiffs' lawyers into a conference room one at a time. We had a short back-and-forth with each one of them trying to get them to give us a reasonable demand. There was some pushback and there was some further back-and-forth, but in the end the total of the demands made by the plaintiffs' lawyers was less than the pot that they were making claims against. When we got to the end of this process, we notified the plaintiffs' lawyers that all of their demands could be met, and we were willing to settle everything. They readily agreed.

Drafting the settlement agreement in this case actually turned out to be more difficult than anything else. When we finally had it done and signed, I volunteered to walk the agreement over to Judge Patterson's chambers to let him know that the case did not need to be tried. I told him why I was there. He told me that he already knew why I was there and that he had learned that the process we used was my idea. He thanked me for my involvement and said to me that he "owed me one". I thought he was kidding. It was an unusual thing for a judge to say. I was too green and naïve to think he meant it.

It wasn't long after that that I learned the inaugural season of the television show Survivor was looking for contestants. The concept of the show appealed to me. I had no idea that it would become the soap opera show that it became. I thought it would be a true survival contest. Confident in my abilities and skills to survive in the wilderness, I decided to apply. If accepted, I would have had to be on set, or at least away from my home and office, for about six weeks. This would be an unusually long period of time for a trial lawyer to be away from the court system.

I knew that Judge Patterson was still the administrative judge and I decided to go see him and ask if he would protect me from being called for any trials, in the unlikely event that I was chosen for the show. He told me he would do it on one condition. I sat silent, waiting on his condition. He told me he would only protect me if I got him an application too. I agreed. We shook hands and I had the sense that he had no intention of signing up for the show. It was just his way of giving me back the "one" he claimed he owed me.

A dump truck driver worked a shift from midnight until 8

a.m. He was involved in one of the strangest accidents I've ever heard of. He was on his way to work late one night on Highway 153 between I-85 and Easley, South Carolina. It is a four-lane highway, separated by a grass median. While on his way to work, without any warning whatsoever, a person ran out of the median right in front of his car. He could not avoid contact and when he hit this person, she smashed into the windshield and then was thrown up over the car. He slammed on his brakes and came to a stop as quickly as he could.

As he started to get out of the car to see what happened, a man came running at him across the grass median, screaming at him. My client got back into his car and sped off. He stopped at the first gas station he came to (this was before cell phones) and called the police. The dispatcher instructed him to return to the scene and an officer would meet him there.

When he arrived back at the scene of the incident, the man who had previously been running at him was placing the body of a woman into the back seat of a vehicle on the side of the road that my client had not previously seen. He rolled down his window and shouted to the man that the police were on their way and he should just wait there. The man ignored him and once he got the woman's body in the car, he closed the back door, got into the car, and drove off.

Shortly after the guy left, the police arrived. My client told them the story and while he was relating the story to them, there was another call on their radios indicating that a man was on I-85 jumping out in front of traffic. One of the officers took off at a high rate of speed to see what was going on there.

As it turned out, the man on I-85 was the same guy who had left the scene of the incident involving my client, with the body. Apparently, the man had intended to take the woman to the hospital in Greenville, but instead of turning north on I-85 towards Greenville, he turned south. He then ran out of gas almost as soon as he got on the interstate. He was extremely intoxicated. When he couldn't get anyone to stop to help him, he pulled the woman's body out of the car and propped her up against the back of the car hoping that would cause someone to take notice and stop. When that didn't work, he decided to start jumping into the lanes of traffic waving his arms trying to get someone to stop.

The police quickly surmised that this was the man who had left the accident scene. The man's story was that he and this woman were out on a date, and both were drinking heavily. They had gotten into an argument in the car. She was driving. He was berating her for something and while they were travelling down the four lane highway towards Easley, she had apparently had enough, so she pulled over onto the right shoulder of the road, opened her door, got out, and started walking across the lanes of traffic and the grass median. The man got out chased her down. The evidence showed that they had an altercation in the grass median. She broke away from him and as she was running back to their car, my client's car struck her.

My client was not charged with any traffic or criminal offense.

The reason I was involved was the woman's estranged husband filed a wrongful death lawsuit against the man she was with and my client. The estranged husband had recently gotten out of prison where he was incarcerated because he had beaten his own brother to death with a piece of pipe for cheating in a card game.

The first time I saw this estranged husband was at a

deposition that had been planned of the boyfriend of the deceased woman. The estranged husband was the scariest human being I've ever encountered. He looked like a caricature of the meanest prisoner in a 1950's prison movie. He arrived at the deposition wearing a very large winter coat, which was strange because it was the middle of the summer. The lawyer for the boyfriend indicated that he and his client were not going to go forward with the deposition unless it was held at the courthouse where everyone would have to pass through a metal detector. The estranged husband got very angry. He got even angrier when his lawyer agreed to this scenario.

So, we all reconvened at the courthouse on the same day, and the estranged husband appeared there without the winter coat.

Every moment in that case was tense. I was able to get my client dismissed from the lawsuit because he had done nothing wrong. Just prior to him being dismissed, the lawyer for the estranged husband called me one day and indicated that his client said that someone was going to die if he didn't get lots of money. The lawyer pleaded with me to offer something on behalf of my client to settle the case. I felt sorry for the lawyer, but told him that I had no authority to settle the case. He told me that he was afraid if he didn't win the case the guy might take it out on him. I later learned that the case against the boyfriend was dismissed as well, but I never heard if the estranged husband exacted any revenge on anybody.

I was involved in a case in which a car wreck in Greenville was witnessed by an engineer who lived in Germany. It became increasingly clear that his testimony was critical in the case. Therefore, both sides were interested in deposing him. In addition to the time difference, we had to get on his busy calendar.

On the day his deposition was scheduled, we called his office in Germany, only to learn that they had forgotten about it and it wasn't on his calendar. His assistant offered to forward the call to his cell phone, and we readily agreed.

When he answered his phone, he was surprised to hear from us, but he agreed to go forward with the deposition while, he informed us, he was driving on the autobahn in Germany.

While the other lawyers in the case were quizzing him about

the facts of the wreck, I was daydreaming about driving on the autobahn. One of my many quirks is I love to drive fast. The thought of driving on a highway with no speed limit appealed to me on a base level.

When they finished their minutiae about the case, I informed the witness that I only had one question for him: "How fast are you driving right now?" The engineer asked me how that was relevant to the case. I conceded it wasn't, it was just my idle curiosity.

He refused to answer my question. I was annoyed. The other lawyers then went around the table asking another round of questions that had no merit except that they were important to the case.

When it got back around to me, I pressed the engineer on my crucial inquiry about his speed. Again, he refused to answer the question. I began thinking about arguments I could make to a judge to compel him to answer the question, but I kept coming up short. I finally relented and said, "No more questions".

EXHIBIT 5 - WALHALLA

Many of those insurance defense trials in the first two years of my career occurred in Walhalla, a small town in the very northwest corner of South Carolina. I loved trying cases there. For some reason, that town produced some unusual juries and trials…

In one case, a young lady who was selected for the jury had been the most recent centerfold in Playboy magazine. My opposing counsel did not do a very good job of hiding his obsession with this young lady. I don't remember much about her… except that she wore a burgundy cardigan, she sat on the front row, second from the left, and the articles in that month's edition were not very interesting.

I tried another case there in which a husband and wife were seated on the jury at the same time. They sat right beside each other in the jury box. I'd never seen this before, and the lawyers joked during the trial about how their participation might increase or decrease the chances of a hung jury and the potential consequences if the jury was not able to reach a unanimous verdict.

When the South Carolina Supreme Court allowed television cameras in courtrooms for the first time, it also allowed radio to broadcast trials. I happened be up for trial on the Monday when the local radio station in Walhalla decided to broadcast a trial live. The station didn't care what the trial was about, they just thought it was a historic moment that they could do so. It was a simple wreck case. But it was unusual because we had to keep taking breaks so that the radio technician could move microphones around to, I guess, optimize the experience for the station's listeners.

One of the most unusual occurrences I ever saw in a courtroom happened in Walhalla. At first blush, it seemed like a relatively straightforward wreck case. However, the plaintiff and defendant told two diametrically opposed stories. The incident involved the plaintiff laying down his motorcycle on a highway because he thought there was going to be a collision with the defendant's vehicle. The plaintiff's story and the defendant's story were like ships passing in the night. It could only have happened one way or the other, there was no middle ground or gray area.

I represented the defendant, a very meek elderly woman.

During the pretrial phase, the plaintiff was represented by a lawyer named Brad Norton, who I came to like very much. Brad was an associate at his law firm. He knew what he was doing, and I expected him to try the case.

When I appeared for trial, I was surprised to see Brad's partner (boss) in court and he indicated to the judge that he would be trying the case. Brad was present, but apparently was going to be sitting second chair.

When it was time for the opening statements, Brad's boss rose, walked over in front of the jury, and *gave my client's version of the accident* as if that was the plaintiff's story. I was as shocked as Brad was. When I looked over at him, he just put his head straight down on the counsel table.

I let the plaintiff's lawyer go on and on about how this wreck had occurred, smiling the whole time to the jury.

When he finished, I rose to give my opening statement. I walked over in front of the jury box and said, "Ladies and gentlemen, as the judge told you a few minutes ago, my name is David Flowers. I represent the defendant. I agree with everything that lawyer just said." I went and sat down, noticing a confused look from the judge as I passed the bench.

As the trial proceeded, it became evident to everyone in the room the mistake that the plaintiff's lawyer had made his opening statement. So, at the end of the trial, when it was time for him to give his closing argument, he said to the jury, "Obviously, I was mistaken in my opening statement." Several members of the jury either laughed out loud or nodded their heads emphatically.

Some judges like to threaten lawyers with contempt citations or even jail from time to time. The closest I ever came to going to jail was when I was appearing in front of a judge I never expected to hear that from. The Honorable Howard Ballenger presided in Walhalla. I always got along with him very well. He was a decent man with a good heart and a good trial judge. In one case however, he spent two days constantly threatening me with jail. It was a convoluted case in which the plaintiff's lawyers had settled the liability portion of the defendant's policy and were trying to present a claim against their client's own underinsured coverage. The problem was the lawyers had not exhausted all of the available liability coverage. At that time there were other jurisdictions in the country that permitted an insured to proceed against their underinsured coverage if they obtained a substantial portion of the available liability coverage, but not necessarily all of it.

South Carolina required the insured to exhaust, or get, all of the available liability coverage before they could proceed against their own underinsured coverage. The plaintiff's lawyers were interested in changing this aspect of insurance law in South Carolina. The problem they created for themselves was that they not only did not exhaust the defendant's liability coverage, they settled for only half of it. So arguably, they did not even get a substantial portion of the liability coverage. They were going to be asking the South Carolina Supreme

Court to go even further than those other jurisdictions.

The underinsured carrier (the plaintiff's own insurance company) refused to step in and accept the defense of the case when my client's carrier tendered it. So, with the dual responsibilities of providing coverage *and* providing a defense, I had to stay on as counsel for the defendants. They were an elderly couple who I liked very much.

The underinsured carrier was represented by Phil Reeves, an outstanding lawyer who I respected and admired. Phil indicated to me before the trial even began that, regardless of what happened during the trial, his instructions from his carrier were that he was not to accept the tender of the defense or participate in the trial in any manner. Therefore, I had an ethical responsibility to defend my clients. I did it to prevent the possibility of a large judgment being obtained against them and potentially imperiling their personal assets.

At the beginning of the trial, Judge Ballenger was confused as to why I was there since my client's carrier had already settled with the plaintiff. I explained to him the difficult position that I was in, and that my clients were in, because of the position of the underinsured carrier not accepting the tender of the defense. Judge Ballenger liked settling cases, like most judges do. He suggested that if I left the case, it would put pressure on the underinsured carrier to settle the case. I politely told him I couldn't leave, because that would leave my clients exposed and without counsel while the plaintiff's counsel tried the case against them.

Phil explained to the judge the instructions he had received from his carrier. So, we began the trial.

It was a tense trial not only because of the underlying insurance issues, but some of the allegations that had been made against my clients were unwarranted and unnecessary. On the first day, during each break, Judge Ballenger would strongly suggest that I leave so that he could put pressure on the underinsured carrier to settle. In response to each of his entreaties, I told him I just could not do that. As the trial wore on, Judge Ballenger got increasingly frustrated with me. His frustration eventually turned into anger, which was very uncharacteristic of him in my experience. On Day 2, I was on my feet arguing a particular evidentiary point when he had had enough. He took a notebook that was in his lap and slammed it down on the bench and said, "That's it! I'm tired of this. I am ordering you to either leave this courtroom right now, or I'm going to put you in jail for contempt of court. Do you understand me?" I was already on my feet, so I just looked down at the counsel table for a moment and as I paused, one of my clients whispered, "David, please leave. We don't want to see you go to jail. We'll be fine."

I looked over at them and whispered, "No, I can't."

At that moment, I really thought I was going to jail. I looked back up at the judge, and said, "With all due respect, Your Honor, I can't leave this courtroom. I can't leave my clients without counsel. I have an ethical responsibility to them."

Judge Ballenger was very angry. I had never seen him like that before. After staring at me for a couple minutes, trying to figure out what he was going to do. He said, "Let's take a break."

During the break, Phil apologized to me and told me he didn't want to see me go to jail either, but he had his instructions. I understood his position, and actually agreed that Phil could not take over the defense. Also, during the break, the judge summoned counsel to his chambers where he continued to threaten to put me in jail.

At the end of Day 2, the judge instructed me to bring a toothbrush to court the next day if I still intended to disobey his direct order to leave his courtroom. I didn't sleep much that night, and my fear of jail started turning into anger toward the judge. He understood the position I was in.

The next morning, the judge asked what I was going to do. I told him I was going to defend my clients. Surprisingly, we proceeded with the trial with no more threats of jail.

In the end, the jury's verdict for the plaintiff did not even exceed the available liability coverage, so there was no opportunity for the plaintiff's lawyers to appeal the case and change the law.

Phil did, however, let me know that he had my back the whole time. He showed me a brand-new toothbrush that he had brought to court for me in case I forgot to bring my own.

As a young lawyer, like most lawyers, I was sometimes put in uncomfortable positions in which I didn't know what to do. In law school they teach you some of what the law is, but more about how to find the law. The real world gives you a much better legal education than any law school. One of the things I was not prepared for by law school or anything else in my experience up to that point happened in Walhalla.

The judge's chambers in the Walhalla courthouse had a bathroom right off of the judge's office. In that bathroom high up on the wall, between the toilet and the sink, there was a vent. On the other side of that vent was the jury's deliberation room. I discovered this in one of my first trials in Walhalla in a very unorthodox way.

It seems that a particular judge enjoyed listening to the jury's deliberations and the judge would "invite" counsel to join him in his bathroom to listen in on the deliberations. I learned about this "invitation" from a more senior lawyer who tried a lot of cases in Walhalla. He indicated to me that the judge expected lawyers to join him because, he thought, that way everybody was in on it so nobody could complain about him doing it.

So, there I was in a very surreal moment huddled in a half

bath while the judge sat on a toilet (lid down) with my opposing counsel and me standing shoulder to shoulder in a tiny bathroom, listening to the jury deliberate.

Conventional wisdom says most juries spend a lot of time talking about the lawyers and the judge. In this case, that was certainly true. But unlike most other cases, in this case the lawyers and judge heard every word of it.

X-rays are fairly ubiquitous exhibits in personal injury cases. I was involved in a case in Walhalla in which the plaintiff's counsel tried something I'd never seen. Instead of trying to introduce an X-ray, he wanted to introduce as an exhibit a positive image of an X-ray. So, where in a normal X-ray, the background is dark and the bones and other bodily structures are a light color, in this positive image the background was white, and the bones and other structures were dark.

The lawyer argued that the positive image showed his client's injuries more clearly and it would be helpful for the jury to see it.

After looking at the image, I thought he had a pretty good point. But, of course, I couldn't agree with that assertion. I raised an objection on the grounds that he had not provided the positive image to me in discovery and I was seeing it for the first time in the courtroom.

We then engaged in a rather lengthy and at times bizarre argument about positives and negatives in photography. It was mostly lighthearted, but as it became clear that the judge was not going to allow the positive image into evidence the plaintiff's lawyer became quite agitated. After a lengthy argument, the judge sustained my objection and did not allow the positive image into evidence. So, the lawyer pulled out a regular X-ray and introduced that instead.

EXHIBIT 6 - LAWYERS

I am not a fan of all lawyers. That has nothing to do with the profession itself. I think practicing law is one of the most noble professions one can enter. I believe that civil juries are the most effective vehicles for change in our society. Lawyers who represent their respective clients zealously and ethically are alright by me. I also hold in the highest regard lawyers who devote their careers to working for change or to representing the downtrodden. What I am not a fan of is lawyers who are lazy (far too many) and those who are more interested in making money than in making a difference. Nevertheless, they are a very entertaining bunch…

I was attending a continuing legal education seminar in Chicago about sexual harassment in the workplace. It was being presented in a large ballroom of a nice hotel. On the first morning, during the first speaker's remarks, a question was asked from the back of the room. I turned to see who was asking the question, and as I did, I recognized an older gentleman sitting right behind me as being a lawyer from Greenville. I had never met him, but I knew who he was because he had been involved in politics. We made eye contact. Apparently, he knew who I was as well, and we quietly shook hands and introduced ourselves to each other for the first time.

Soon after the brief exchange, there was a break in the seminar. During the break, he asked if I had any plans for the evening. I told him that I always liked to see Blue Man Group whenever I visited Chicago. He asked what that was. I told him that the only way I could explain it was that it was an assault on your senses… like a vaudeville act on steroids. He seemed intrigued. I asked if he would be interested in joining me. He said he would, so during the next break, I was able to get him a ticket.

We had lunch together and got to know each other a little bit. We were both staying in the hotel that hosted the seminar, so that evening we shared a cab to the theater to see the show.

When we arrived at the theater, after presenting our tickets, we were issued rain ponchos. (Go see the show and sit in the first five rows.) He gave me a weird look and said, "You didn't mention anything about wearing a poncho." I just laughed and ushered him to our seats.

I had seen the show many times before, so I mostly just watched his reaction to the experience. I'm quite certain that he had never seen anything like it.

In the cab on the way back to the hotel, he raved about it. We hung out in the hotel bar for a bit, talking about mutual acquaintances and telling war stories.

The next morning, as I walked into the seminar room, he was waiting for me to arrive. He approached, shook my hand and said, "David, I really enjoyed that show last night. I want to repay you. Let me take care of the entertainment tonight." I asked what he had in mind. He indicated that he had not yet decided, but he would try to make it as good as the night before. I agreed to join him, because I had no other plans.

We spent some time together during the breaks that day and in spite of my inquiries, he never let on what he had planned for the evening. At the end of the day, he told me to meet him in the hotel bar at 7:00.

When I arrived in the bar that evening at 7:00 sharp, I noticed that he was chatting with two beautiful women. I had heard that he was something of a lady's man, so I assumed that he was just chatting and flirting with them while he waited on me to arrive. He introduced me to the women. Instead of us taking our leave and going somewhere else to do something, he informed me that the ladies were going to be joining us. He leaned closer to the one next to him and the other put her hands on me. I froze. It became very clear, very quickly, that the ladies were professionals. I assumed that he had engaged them to be our "entertainment" for the evening.

I was still quite naïve, and my mind immediately started racing, trying to figure out how I was going to get out of this situation. After a minute or so, and just as the bartender put my beer on the bar, I said to my colleague, "Can I speak to you in private for a minute?"

We both excused ourselves from the ladies and walked into the lobby of the hotel. I told him, "I can't do this, I'm married!"

He replied, "So? I am too."

I was stunned by his answer. I remembered feeling like the

country bumpkin in the big city. I could tell that this was not the first time that he had participated in this activity. I told him that I could not do it and needed to beg off. He was quite annoyed with me, insinuating that he had already incurred great expense. I told him that I was sorry for that, but I would not be joining them.

I went back into the bar and told the women that I was not feeling well and that, unfortunately, I would not be very good company that night, so I excused myself and went up to my room.

The next morning, as I walked into the seminar room, he was waiting for me again. He made a beeline for me. I was a little surprised that he was moving toward me, and I expected another unpleasant comment about how much he had spent on the previous evening.

Instead of what I expected, as he got near me, a big smile came across his face and he stuck out his hand. As I shook his hand, he said, “David, I cannot thank you enough for what you did for me last night.” The smile did not leave his face the entire day.

For years thereafter, every time I saw him in Greenville, he would shake my hand and thank me again.

During my time at Ness Motley, I was involved in a case against a major corporation which had a manufacturing facility in a small town in the South. We represented 240 plaintiffs. My co-counsel was one of the best lawyers I've ever worked with, and she was also quite a free spirit.

We spent so much time in this town that our firms rented two houses and an office in the downtown area. We had a witness come to the office one day who disclosed some confidential information to us. We were quite surprised a couple of weeks later when the defense lawyer mentioned this information to us. We became suspicious that the defense lawyers and/or their client might be listening in on our conversations at our office. There was also a conversation that I had had at my rented house, in the living room, which the defense lawyer also seemed to be knowledgeable about.

My co-counsel and I decided to see if we were crazy. We had a conversation in the office one day where we mentioned a fictitious witness. We then had the same conversation at the rented houses. We were shocked when a few days later one of the defense lawyers asked us about this person. We were then convinced that they were listening to our conversations.

We met away from the house and the office to discuss how we would proceed. Because of the nature of the size and complexity of litigation the Ness Motley was routinely involved in, the firm had a pretty sophisticated security department. When I reported to my supervisor what we suspected, he sent a security person to the town the very next day.

We met the security person at the office first and he swept the room with some electronic devices. We are all startled when one of the devices registered a positive indication on one of the office chairs. It seemed to confirm our suspicions. After he finished the sweep of the entire office, he went back and focused on that chair. In the end, it turned out to be a false positive.

We then went to the house where I was staying. The security person swept the house with the same electronic devices and found nothing. However, he seemed interested in a huge plate glass window in the living room. He asked me where we had had the conversation in the house. I told him in that very living room. He then walked outside the house. There were woods abutting the backyard. He disappeared into the woods for a few minutes.

He returned and came straight up to me and said, "They are indeed listening to you."

I asked him what he was talking about. He found an area in the backyard in the woods that was beaten down and looked like someone had been there for quite some time. He informed me that there is technology in which you point a laser at a glass window and listen to conversations on the inside.

We spent the rest of that case pretending to be James Bond and being careful not to discuss sensitive matters in the houses or the office.

In the same case, the defense firm was one of the largest firms in the world and the lead lawyer was an outstanding lawyer who I came to respect greatly. Early in the case there was a moment which

I still chuckle about today. This lawyer was very refined, very polished, and came from a long line of lawyers. He always attended depositions in a suit and tie. My co-counsel and I attended depositions in jeans and casual wear, and she sometimes wore cowboy boots.

In one of the earliest depositions in the case, the defense lawyer was deposing one of our clients, and I was seated right next to the client. My co-counsel was seated down at the end of the table, some 8 or 10 feet away. At one point in the deposition, my co-counsel leaned back in her chair and put her feet up on the table and crossed her legs. I could see that this bothered the defense lawyer. I'm pretty sure he had never seen anything like this in a deposition in his career.

After a few minutes, when he was in the middle of a question, my co-counsel put her entire lower legs up on the table and crossed them. He stopped in the middle of a question, did not look down the table, did not look at me, kept his eyes on our client, but you could just see the fabric of his reality being ripped apart. He was quiet for a long awkward moment.

I finally said, "Is something wrong?" He didn't even acknowledge my question. He just finished his question to the witness, picking up exactly where he had paused, and acted as if nothing ever happened.

Gregg and I were contacted by a father whose four sons had all been molested by a Catholic priest in Chicago. The father was looking for a lawyer to represent his family against the church in Chicago. I was on vacation with my family at the time, but I agreed to take the call and we spent about an hour on the phone with the father.

At the end of the conversation, the father asked Gregg and me if we would be opposed to working with another lawyer on the case. We told him that we would entertain the idea and wanted to know who the other lawyer might be. He told us it was Johnnie Cochran, O.J. Simpson's former lawyer. The father told us that he was interested in having Johnnie Cochran represent them, but he liked the phone call he had with us and wanted to know if we would all work together. I remained silent for the rest of the call.

As soon as we hung up with the father, I called Gregg and told him that if he was interested in handling the case with Johnnie Cochran, he had my blessing, but I did not want anything to do with Cochran. He was clearly a good lawyer, but I think his conduct in the O.J. Simpson trial was a disgrace and I had no interest in being involved in any case with him.

Gregg tried to persuade me that it might be interesting to handle this case with Cochran. I told him I thought Johnnie Cochran would see us as his assistants, that we would do all of the work, and he would take all the credit. I told him I wasn't interested in being Johnnie Cochran's assistant or anything else.

Gregg asked if I would just listen to him. I relented and said to Gregg that if he set up a call, I would hear what Cochran had to say. Gregg arranged a call. It was to occur only a couple of days later. It was scheduled for 10:15 a.m., west coast time, Cochran's office was to initiate the call.

Gregg and I waited by our phones. The appointed hour came and went. We waited longer. Finally, at about 10:45, west coast time, Gregg called Cochran's office in Los Angeles. He was informed that

Cochran had taken the day off and would not be in the office. I was really annoyed. I told Gregg I was not interested in talking to *or about* Cochran anymore.

He later told me that Cochran called him the next day and wanted to talk about getting us in the case. He told Gregg that he had not handled any sex abuse cases, but "he heard we were good at it and he wanted to learn from us". (Yeah, right.) Gregg again pitched to me the idea of working with Cochran. I still said no.

Less than a week later, I saw Cochran on TV talking about his vast experience in representing victims of sexual abuse. It confirmed what I already thought about the guy. Gregg ended up declining to get involved in the case in Chicago.

I was once involved with a coalition of lawyers who handled some litigation related to the national tobacco litigation. We decided to take on not only the tobacco companies, but also the attorneys general who were negotiating what we saw as a sweetheart deal for the states and the tobacco companies, but a horrible deal for the victims of tobacco.

At one meeting where the lawyers from all of the firms involved in this project were sitting around a conference table, someone mentioned that if we were successful there would likely be billions of dollars in fees to be divided among the lawyers. This initiated a rather surreal discussion about what each lawyer intended to do if we were able to recover billions of dollars.

Some of the responses were rather fanciful, some were noble. For example, one lawyer I really respected said that he would form an environmental law firm to do what he could to protect wilderness areas in his home state of North Carolina. Others spoke of cars, houses, travel, the usual perks that would come with that kind of money.

When it was my turn and someone asked what I would intend to do with my share, I merely said "If we ever get that kind of money, I defy any of you to find me."

A common ploy of lawyers is to put the other side in the

position of having to prove a negative. As anyone who knows anything about logic is aware, this is a very difficult position to be in. But I learned a wonderful response whenever anyone tried to put me in the position of proving a negative and it came from an outstanding lawyer in Greenville named Johnny Peace. A lawyer was putting Johnny in this difficult position and Johnny's very measured reply was, "Well, I can't prove that blue whales don't speak French at the bottom of the ocean, but I'm pretty sure they don't."

Frank Eppes is a well-known and well-respected lawyer and a good friend. "Little Frank" is a big man, approximately 6' 11". He did a lot of criminal work. I went upstairs to his office one day to ask him a question. He was standing in the door of his office with two huge stacks of cash in his gargantuan hands. The cash was very neatly stacked and had rubber bands around it. The stacks had to have been 8 inches tall each. He told me before he would answer my question, he had one for me.

With one stack of this currency in each hand, and gesticulating dramatically with those stacks, he asked very slowly,

"Do you think there is any truth to the allegation that my client is a drug dealer?"

There was a lawyer in Charlotte who had a well-deserved reputation of being the biggest asshole lawyer in the Carolinas. Gregg and I had filed a case in North Carolina, in a county near Charlotte. This clown showed up as counsel for the defendant. Early on in the case, he wrote in a very condescending letter that dealing with us was like dealing with a tag-team wrestling team.

One of my other quirks is that I sew. I learned to do it in order to make my own outdoor gear, like sleeping bags, backpacks and rain gear.

So, I made Gregg and me some wrestling masks out of some stretchy material and decorated mine with a hammer on the forehead and his with a scalpel, because I liked bashing heads, and he was an expert at cutting off important pieces of anatomy of unsuspecting lawyers and witnesses without them realizing it.

I looked forward to an opportunity for us to wear these

masks for that jerk, but he withdrew from the case before we ever had a chance.

Damn it!

I had a reputation for saying just about anything to anybody and was known to use the F-bomb more than I probably should have.

In one particular settlement conference there were six lawyers arrayed down the opposite side of the table. They were uninterested in settling the case. They were also being quite condescending and demeaning with respect to my client and me. I finally had my fill of it.

I asked my client to step out of the room to discuss something. Once in the hallway, I asked him to wait in a separate conference room while I went back and spoke to the lawyers.

I re-entered the conference room where the lawyers were awaiting our return. Their conversation stopped immediately. I started at the left end of the table, pointed at the lawyer, and said, "Fuck you". Then I pointed at the next lawyer and said, "Fuck you.".

And then the next one and then the next one and then the next one and added some extra gusto with the last one. I then walked out of the room to retrieve my client and we left.

Later that day I got a phone call from one of the lawyers. They finally made a reasonable offer and we were able to settle the case soon thereafter.

I was involved briefly in a case involving a scout troop that was composed of special needs boys. It was a serious case with allegations that the scoutmaster had sexually molested some of the scouts. I was hired to represent one of the scouts. When we made the allegation, not only did the scoutmaster deny the allegation, but he and his wife lashed out at the scout that I represented and accused him of stealing money from a fundraiser the troop had been involved in.

The young man that I represented was devastated by this allegation because he had not stolen any money and he was upset that he was being accused of doing so.

As the case continued, the scoutmaster's own son disclosed that he too was a victim of his father's sexual deviancy. The wife of the scoutmaster, as any mother would be expected to do, believed her son, and supported him.

However, she continued to assert that my client was lying and continued to accuse him of stealing money. She was represented by a friend of mine, Jim Walsh. When I arrived at Jim's office to take her deposition, he asked to speak with me in private.

Once we were in his office, he disclosed to me that his client had stage IV cancer and was close to death. He asked me to take it easy on her. I told him I did not know that she was sick and that my conduct in the deposition would be dictated entirely by his client's testimony.

During the deposition, the woman went out of her way to disparage my young client and continuously accused him of stealing the money. She also accused him of lying about being molested, even though she believed her own son.

I was pretty annoyed by this and apparently let it show

because during a break Jim said to me, "I can't believe you are being so rough on a woman who is dying."

I told him, "I don't care if she is dying, she is lying about a special needs kid and I'm not gonna tolerate it."

After the case was over Jim used to tell the story to other lawyers in my presence and kid me about beating up on a woman who was dying. I would always follow his story with whatever I might've done to her paled in comparison to what she was saying about my client.

I have a few regrets from my career, but the way I conducted myself in that deposition is not one of them.

I had another case with Jim Walsh that was bizarre on many levels. It involved a doctor in Greenville who would prescribe addictive medications for his female patients. Once they were hooked on the meds, he would demand sexual favors for future prescriptions. (I came to learn that this was more common than the public knows. I had several of these cases in my career.)

This particular doctor, when I encountered him, was 82 years old.

One of my clients, who was a patient of his, was concerned that no one would believe her regarding the sexual allegations. So, she decided to get some corroborating evidence. She went to the doctor's office one day to get her prescription. While there, she took a series of photographs, all with his consent, of him writing her a prescription on his prescription pad.

Then, she took a second series of photographs, again *all with his consent*, of him standing in the hallway of his office with his pants unzipped and his… ahem… "manhood" sticking out of his pants. He had one of his arms across his eyes expecting that no one could identify the person in the photographs as him. However, he was wearing the same clothes, including a distinctive tie, in the other series of photos at his desk.

She brought the photos to me. I had copies of them loaded onto a CD and sent them to Jim. He called me the next day and rather loudly said, "Don't you ever send me anything like this again!"

I started laughing and said, "Just think about it, Jim, we're now in an exclusive club: we've both seen an 82-year-old penis."

He didn't think it was very funny.

So, I followed up with, "AND, the only *other* members of our exclusive club are your client's patients!"

In that same case, Jim Walsh called me one day and asked if I knew about my client's criminal record. I told him I did not. He would not tell me what he knew. He just said, "you better check it out."

I did some research and discovered that my client had been arrested for solicitation of prostitution. I went to Pickens County to get the file so I could see what the case was about. There, I learned that while in the Pickens County jail, one of the inmates offered up some evidence to the deputies to try to help his own situation. He alleged that he knew a woman who ran an escort service in the county. The deputies were interested, so they set up a recording device on a phone line and had the guy call my client. He told her he was in jail but was interested in her services. They did not discuss details on the call, but she agreed to go to the jail for further, uh, discussions.

She arrived at the jail shortly thereafter and asked to see him. She was taken to his cell where, through the bars of the cell, she and he discussed services she was willing to provide *through the bars of the jail cell!*

Yep… you guessed it… the deputies were recording every word of it.

I. Could. Not. Make. This. Stuff. Up.

There was a young lawyer in our building who had recently returned home to Greenville from Washington DC, where he had served on the staff of a United States Senator. I genuinely liked him a lot and took him under my wing, trying to give guidance whenever he asked, and sometimes when he didn't.

He had one quirk that drove me crazy. It was a quirk that I had seen in many other people who had served on congressional staffs before. It seems to me that everyone who goes to Washington to work in Congress and comes back home, takes credit for everything that goes on in that congressional office during their tenure, no matter high or low on the totem pole they were in the office or whether they were even involved.

This particular young man had the unfortunate predilection of claiming, whenever someone mentioned a federal statute, that he drafted the statute being discussed while he was working for the senator. Everyone in the building knew it wasn't true, but we tolerated it because we liked him.

One Friday afternoon, there were several lawyers hanging out in my office, which was a fairly common occurrence on Friday afternoons. We were all just winding down, swapping stories, doing what lawyers do.

When I had the floor, I was sharing with them some recent events in a case Gregg and I were working on that involved the False Claims Act, a federal statute that permits individual citizens to bring a lawsuit, under certain circumstances, to recover money or other assets that have been obtained by someone else through fraud on the federal government. The case Gregg and I had involved a contract on a nuclear submarine. It was a big case. The contract involved more than $4 billion.

When I first mentioned the False Claims Act, this young lawyer announced to the room that he had drafted that statute when he was working for the senator. I knew it wasn't true, but I let it go.

When I got to the end of the story, he wanted to emphasize the fact that he drafted the statute. So, he started talking about the time that he drafted it. I interrupted him and asked, "Are you sure you drafted that statute?"

He replied that he had.

I had reached my limit, so I said, "Well that's funny, because *President Lincoln* signed it during the Civil War."

The room erupted in laughter. I didn't want to embarrass him. I was just tired of his insistence that every federal statute had been drafted by him.

I explained to him that the statute had been drafted to stop war profiteering almost 150 years before he was born. He then walked it back a little bit and said he meant to say that he had drafted some amendments to the statute.

My response was that he should just stop doing that. I think he took it to heart because I don't recall him ever taking credit for drafting a federal statute after that Friday afternoon.

We remained friends and I still think he is a fine lawyer and one of the most decent human beings I have ever met.

I was asked one day, by a good friend, to get involved in a case in which a tangential matter turned out to be much more that I bargained for. He and another lawyer were representing a woman in a lawsuit against Walmart. She had slipped and fallen in one of their stores and sustained an injury.

While my friend was representing her, she was in a different Walmart shopping one day and, as she left the store, she was accosted in the parking lot by a representative of Walmart who accused her of shoplifting. He asked her to return to the store, which she did. She denied that she was shoplifting and produced a receipt.

The receipt was taken from her, ostensibly to make a photocopy if it, but was not returned.

When the police came, she was charged with shoplifting. She kept telling the police she had a receipt for the merchandise and the Walmart representatives denied it.

When she appeared in court to defend herself on the shoplifting charge, she told the judge that she had a receipt that was taken from her by Walmart employees. A Walmart representative was there at the hearing and denied that she had purchased the items that she was accused of shoplifting. The woman was found guilty of shoplifting.

A couple weeks after she was found guilty, she received in the mail a plain manila envelope, with no return address, that contained a photocopy of the receipt. She took it to her lawyer, who then called me. He asked me to get involved for the limited purpose of getting her shoplifting conviction overturned based on the receipt.

I agreed to get involved and drafted a motion to reopen the criminal case alleging that Walmart had hidden the receipt and therefore a fraud had been perpetrated on the court.

When I went to the magistrate's office to file the motion, the magistrate happened to be standing in the foyer of the court. He asked me what I was there for. I explained to him about the conviction and the receipt being mailed anonymously. He invited me back to his chambers. He read the motion, looked at the receipt, and said he believed an injustice had been done.

I told him I would make myself available if he wanted to schedule a hearing if either the prosecutor's office or Walmart wanted to contest it. He said he saw no need for that, and he signed an order overturning her conviction on the spot.

I drove straight to my friend's office and delivered the order.

About a week later, I received in the mail, from another lawyer in town who I knew pretty well, a notice to take my sworn testimony in a deposition. This lawyer was defending Walmart in the slip and fall case that the lady had pending.

I called and asked this lawyer, "Why didn't you just pick up the phone and call me, instead of sending me a notice of deposition?"

He said, "David, we're friends. It is in your best interest and mine that the first time I hear you tell this story you are under oath." That angered me because I did not know what he was insinuating or what was going on.

I appeared for the deposition. He asked me one question. "Tell me what happened."

I then related the story that you read above about my visit to the judge's chambers. He asked no more questions and concluded the deposition. I was even more puzzled than I was before.

A few days later I learned what was going on. The story I related above about the shoplifting and the receipt and receiving this receipt in the mail is what the client had related to her lawyer, my friend. After I got the criminal conviction overturned and my deposition was taken, Walmart produced a receipt that only had a few of the items on it that she was accused of shoplifting that day.

The Walmart lawyer pointed out something that neither my friend nor I had noticed. The receipt that she claimed to have received in the mail had been cut and pasted. The items on the receipt did not even add up to the total amount on the receipt.

The client had been lying all along. She had in fact been shoplifting. And after she was caught, she went back to various Walmarts and bought each of the items that she was accused of shoplifting, which they were able to prove. She then cut and pasted each item from its respective receipt and taped them all together so she had one receipt that purported to be the receipt she claimed she had the day she was accused of shoplifting, taken from her by Walmart, and then later allegedly mailed anonymously to her.

My friend fired her as a client, wrote a letter to the court explaining what happened, and made it clear that neither he nor I had any prior knowledge that she had been lying all along.

The lesson I learned was to never represent anyone I could not look in the eye and hear their story first-hand.

I heard a story once about two lawyers back in the day who really didn't like each other. One of them got the upper hand in a case and he decided he wanted to be mean. He told the other lawyer that he would not settle the case unless he got his opponent's chair. Not just any chair, but the chair from behind the man's desk.

I always loved that story and actually tried to emulate it once.

We were in a settlement conference in a case where we clearly had the upper hand and we knew there was no way that the defense was going to take the case to trial. The settlement conference was taking place at the brand-new offices of the defense firm in Charlotte. They were literally moving in on the day that we were conducting the settlement conference.

The conference room where they parked Gregg and me and our clients was furnished with brand-spanking-new furniture. Some of the chairs still had plastic on them. They were the most amazing chairs I ever sat in. I decided I wanted one of those chairs. And then, for reasons that escape me now, I decided I actually needed two of those chairs.

For the rest of the negotiations I kept demanding two of those chairs as part of any deal. The defense lawyer, an outstanding lawyer named Mel Garofalo, who I liked and respected, thought I was kidding. It took some time before he realized I was serious. Mel told me to go buy my own chairs.

I told him, "I don't want just any chairs, I want *your* chairs." I think he was getting a little aggravated with me.

At the end of the negotiation, we were able to reach an agreement. I said, "We don't have an agreement until I get my chairs." He did not think it was funny and he ignored me.

I never got those damned chairs.

During the same case I was going crazy because I knew that I had met Mel before. And I knew that I had not just met him, but that I'd spent time with him, so I presumed we had had a case together in the past.

Throughout the case, I kept asking him where we knew each other from. He knew the answer, but he wouldn't tell me, which made me only want to know more. He told me when the case was over, he would tell me.

When we finally got the case resolved (without me getting any chairs) and had signed all the appropriate settlement paperwork, I asked him, "Okay, how do we know each other?" He reminded me that he had recruited me and had offered me a job when I graduated from law school.

I felt like a heel.

Shortly after obtaining a jury verdict in excess of $100 million, my next trial was a much needed, and long overdue, humbling experience.

I shared office space with a fairly new lawyer who mostly did real estate closings and was very nervous about being on his feet in a courtroom. He came into my office one afternoon and told me that he had a trial starting the next morning that was pretty straightforward but that he was extremely nervous about trying. He asked me if I would help.

I said I would. I asked him what he wanted me to do. He said he would like for me to do the opening statement. He brought me the file.

After reviewing it, I agreed it was a very straightforward case. His client's vehicle was hit in the rear by another vehicle and she sustained some soft tissue injuries. It seemed like a case I could try in my sleep.

The next morning, we arrived at the courthouse to try the case and I met the defense lawyer, Chris Antley. We picked the jury. I gave a brief opening statement, informing the jury that my client had been struck in the rear and there really was no dispute about who was at fault. I mentioned her injuries but didn't talk about them too much.

When it was Chris' turn, the first words out of his mouth were, "This impact was so slight, there was a baby asleep in the backseat of the plaintiff's car, and the baby did not wake up."

This was news to me. Neither my co-counsel nor our client had mentioned to me that there was a baby in the backseat or that the baby didn't wake up. So, I turned and looked at my co-counsel and whispered, "Is that true?"

He shrugged his shoulders and whispered back, "So?"

I was more than a little perturbed because that is a fact that I would like to have known. Over the course of the trial I think Chris must've said, "The baby didn't wake up" at least 50 times.

I don't begrudge him. I would've done the same thing, but I sure got tired of hearing it. Not surprisingly, the jury returned a defense verdict.

For years after that trial, every time I saw Chris, he reminded me that the baby didn't wake up.

During my divorce proceeding I was represented by a well-respected and universally liked lawyer named Tom Traxler. Tom thought I was offering to give up too much and he kept resisting the offer that I wanted to make to resolve the proceeding. Finally, after a session where he browbeat me unmercifully, he finally said, "Okay, I will agree to convey this offer on one condition."

I asked what that condition was.

He said, "When your divorce from her is final, you have to marry me."

I got a call one day from my friend Lee Plumblee. I knew that he and his partner Frank Eppes had bought a building and their plan was to gather some of the better plaintiff's lawyers in Greenville to be under one roof to not only to share expenses, but to be near each other for consultation and to bounce ideas. Lee asked me to come over to the building to talk about maybe moving over there.

When I arrived, he escorted me into a large conference room at one end of the building which protruded off of the main building. It was a rectangular shaped room with windows on three sides and only one door, back into the main building. As Lee was doing his best to use flattery to persuade me to move into the building, I was sizing up and admiring the conference room we were sitting in.

I was thinking, "*Now, this would make a great office.*" So, when he finished his presentation, I just said, "I'll take this room right here."

Lee chuckled, and said, "No, really."

To which I responded, "No… Really."

Lee stared at me for a couple minutes without saying a word. Finally, with a tone of resignation in his voice, he said, "Alright, let me talk to Frank."

I moved in the following week.

At my children's swim meets (and other social occasions), I always attempted to find a spot off to myself away from the crowd where I would read or catch up on some work. When it was time for my children to swim, I would get up, walk over to the pool, watch them swim, congratulate them, and then head back over to my spot.

On one particular occasion, I was headed to the pool past a group of lawyers who were chatting and one of them, Scott Anderson, a good lawyer and a good guy, said to the rest of the crowd he was talking to, loud enough for me to hear, "There goes everybody's favorite misanthrope, David Flowers."

I just kept walking because I did not know what the term meant. That evening, I looked it up and learned that it means a person who hates people.

The next day, when I got to the office, I wrote Scott a letter which said, "Dear Scott, Yesterday, you referred to me as a misanthrope and I did not know what it meant. Last night I looked it up and learned that it means a person who hates people. I don't hate all people, just most people. And to prove it, I want to take you to lunch."

There was a defense lawyer in Greenville that I got along with well on a personal level but had two separate incidents with him in trials that did not sit well with me, and still don't.

The first time we ever tried a case together, I was representing a gentleman who was injured in an industrial accident when an air hose exploded and blew most of the underside of his upper arm away. He lived in a small town and as he was transported to the hospital, his wife arrived at the loading dock of the hospital about the same time as the ambulance. One of the doctors on duty was a close friend of theirs. The doctor said to my client's wife, "The first thing I'm going to try to do is save his life, and then I'll try to save his arm." The doctors were able to save both his life and his arm, but he was severely disabled thereafter.

In the trial, experts were retained by both sides and it was a well fought trial until my opponent brought out a piece of pipe that I had never seen before. I objected and argued to the judge that the pipe had not been produced in discovery and therefore was not admissible at trial. The defense lawyer told the judge that he had produced the pipe prior to the trial and that I had seen it, which was false. Judges never like to be put in the position of having to make a ruling with one lawyer calling the other dishonest or a liar. I knew this but I was not going to back down because I knew I had never seen the pipe. Unbelievably, the judge ruled that the defense lawyer could use the pipe and show it to the jury. I will never forget the grin the lawyer gave me when the judge ruled in his favor.

The pipe apparently had an impact on the jury because they ruled in the defendant's favor. I was livid and I soon learned that I was not the only lawyer in Greenville who had experienced this tactic by this particular lawyer.

The next time I had to try a case with that same defense lawyer, my client had been in a car accident. His glasses were broken, his briefcase was destroyed, and the EMTs had cut his business suit off of him to render medical care. His own insurance company, which was represented by the same defense lawyer, refused to pay for any of these items or for my client's rental car. My client was not making a personal injury claim. Surprisingly, he only wanted his glasses, his suit, and his briefcase paid for, along with reimbursement for the rental car. It was an insurance company that he had been paying premiums to for years. It seemed silly that they wouldn't pay him, so I filed what is called a bad faith failure to pay case against the insurance company. These cases are a plaintiff lawyer's dream because it is not often that you have an insurance company as a named defendant. In most cases you are not even allowed to mention insurance to the jury. In this case I could not only mention it, but I had the insurance company as the named opposing party.

During the trial, I encountered the same situation with the same lawyer that I had in the previous trial. He pulled out a document that I have never seen before and wanted to enter it into evidence. I objected and told the judge I had never seen the document. Just as he did in the previous trial, the lawyer told the judge that he had shown it to me in discovery. Once again, the judge was in an uncomfortable position.

Not long after that first incident, the defense lawyer produced a transcript of what he said was a recorded statement that my client had given to the insurance company shortly after the accident. In my written discovery requests, I had asked for any recorded statements that the insurance company had in their possession. The defense lawyer had responded *in writing* that the insurance company had no recorded statement of my client, yet he pulled one out of his file at trial and wanted to use it. I showed that written response to the judge who was more than a little annoyed because the defense lawyer had already argued to the judge that he had produced the written statement to me, which meant that he was lying to the judge and the judge knew it. The judge admonished the lawyer and did not allow the recorded statement to come in evidence. The judge then cautioned the lawyer that he had better not attempt to use any other documents that were not produced in discovery.

Not too long after that, on the same day, it happened again.

The lawyer attempted to use a document that had printing on both sides of the paper. In discovery, he had provided a copy of the front of the page, but not the back. Now, in the trial he was trying to introduce information that was on the back of the page. I objected again and I showed the judge the documents that had been produced from the defendant. They were numbered sequentially, and the back of the page was not included in those documents. The judge was livid, and so was I.

I made a motion to strike the defendant's Answer, which is an extreme and unusual sanction, but I thought appropriate for this pattern of misconduct. If granted, it meant that the jury would be instructed that the defendant loses the case and they were only to assess an amount of damages to be awarded to the plaintiff. The judge stated that before he ruled on my motion, we were going to take a break and that the defense lawyer needed to call his client and inform them that the court was considering striking their Answer and that they had better think seriously about settling the case.

During the extended break, the defense lawyer and his client made a couple of offers to my client to settle which were rejected.

When the time came to reconvene in the courtroom, without a settlement, as the judge was entering the courtroom the defense lawyer stepped over to my table and said to me in a whisper, "You need to withdraw this motion because you're making this personal."

I said to him, "I'm not the one making this personal because this is the second time you have put me in this position, and I'm done with you."

The judge sat down at the bench and asked if we had reached a settlement. Unexpectedly, the defense lawyer rose and informed the judge that they had agreed to pay what my client was asking for and therefore the case was settled. I was surprised, and not a little disappointed, that we would not get to hear the jury's verdict. The case was settled for four times more than my client was willing to settle for before the shenanigans at the trial.

I was involved in a case with Sam Mabry, a lawyer in Greenville that I liked and respected very much. It was a contentious case that involved allegations of sexual misconduct by a businessman.

We were able to get the case settled for a figure that was higher than my client expected, and *much* higher than the defendant expected to pay!

After we reached the agreement in principle, we were trying to hammer out the details in a written settlement agreement. During this back and forth about the language in the final document, I was on my way to the men's room when I passed Sam in the hallway. He was leaning against a wall marking up a draft of the document. As I walked past him, he said loud enough for me to hear, "Blackmail, that's what this is."

I stopped, turned around and walked back to Sam and whispered in his ear, "Sam, I don't care what you call it, just make sure you spell my name right on the check."

In a case involving a sexual assault in an education setting, the mediator was an elderly gentleman who was one of the most respected lawyers in Greenville. At the mediation, he was clearly uncomfortable hearing about, and having to talk about, the details of the assault. The victim was a sixteen-year-old girl. She was the only child of her mother. The facts of the case were particularly egregious, especially about how the defendant treated the young girl when she told what had happened to her.

Even though the plaintiffs were quite poor, their demand to settle the case was very modest.

The mediator liked my clients and was surprised at their low expectations. Early on in the discussions, the defendant made an offer that exceeded the plaintiffs' expectations. I thought we were done. I was surprised to learn that we were not.

The mediator asked me to join him in the hallway. He told me that my clients deserved more, and that he was sure that the defendant would pay more… considerably more. He asked if I would permit him to speak to my clients about raising their expectations and them giving him permission to extract as much as he could from the defendant. I agreed to both.

He went back into the room with my clients and made a very impassioned plea to them to let him see what he could get them.

I spent the rest of the day in the conference room with my clients. Periodically, the mediator would come into the room and bring us up to speed on his negotiations with the defense lawyers. I felt like a bump on a log.

Toward the end of the day, the mediator came into the room and announced that the defendant had made what they characterized as a final, FINAL offer. When he disclosed the number, my clients were incredulous. It was more money than they had ever imagined in their lives. They readily accepted.

The mediator, however, was not so anxious. He told them that they were again accepting too quickly. He said that we should spend some time chatting, so he could then go back into the other room and exclaim that the plaintiffs were not satisfied. He intended to tell them that we were "close, but not quite there".

After several minutes, he decided he had taken enough time with us, so he went to see the other side. He returned a while later, with an increased offer.

I was flabbergasted.

He indicated that he thought he had finally gotten all that the defendant might offer, so my clients should settle. Of course, they did.

The mediator was very proud of what he had done for these plaintiffs and he became quite emotional when they expressed their gratitude to him. Lots and lots of tears.

For several years afterwards, every time I saw him, he asked about those clients.

He was one of the most decent lawyers I ever met.

Gregg and I were involved in a defamation case in Charleston which was easily one of the most bizarre cases I was ever involved in. Our client was an executive in the healthcare field. He had been recently divorced from his wife. He was hired to run a brand-new hospital and was excited about the new opportunity.

Just as he was taking the helm at this new position, someone began sending anonymous letters to his friends, family members, and his new employer. The letters contained false allegations that he had engaged in unprofessional conduct, that he had been unfaithful to his wife, and that he had a sexually transmitted disease.

There were some clues that his ex-wife was involved in this scheme, so we brought a defamation action against her. She adamantly denied sending the letters or knowing anything about them.

Several things then happened, all of which were unexpected, and all of which were fairly unique in my career.

First, we sent a subpoena to her Internet Service Provider to get copies of emails which we thought might shed some light on the anonymous letters. The Internet Service Provider had already created a CD with the pertinent emails on it during this couple's divorce proceeding. When Gregg sent the subpoena to the Internet Service Provider, they forwarded him a copy of this CD.

The ex-wife hired a smarmy lawyer in Mount Pleasant who brought a lawsuit against Gregg and me for violating a federal anti-computer hacking statute. The statute was created to prevent people from hacking into servers. We never hacked into anything. We had merely sent a lawful subpoena to an Internet Service Provider. That lawsuit was summarily dismissed.

There were certain breadcrumbs that eventually led us to start looking at our client's ex-father-in-law. Among those breadcrumbs: we were able to intercept one of these anonymous letters before it had been opened by the recipient. We sent the letter to a lab to see if they could obtain any DNA from the envelope. Luckily, they were able to obtain the DNA, and sure enough, the DNA indicated that it was a family member of our client's ex-wife who had licked the envelope.

We then requested access to the ex-wife's father's computer. We knew that he had also been in the healthcare industry but was retired, that he lived in a small town some ways away from Charleston, and that he was very upset when our client left his daughter. We were interested in any communications between this gentleman and his daughter that might shed some light on these anonymous letters.

Instead of just providing us with copies of such emails, we were quite surprised when his lawyer provided to us a forensic copy of the entire hard drive from this gentleman's computer. It contained everything. Not only did we get emails and word-processing documents, we also got logs of his internet activity. It was a treasure trove of information, some related to the case but plenty that was not. However, some of the information that was not related shed new light on the case.

We had learned that this man was a deacon in his church. We knew that he and his wife ran a small business in the town where they lived. We also knew that he spent many evenings in a workshop located above their business building and repairing lamps as a hobby. When we looked at the logs of his Internet activity, we discovered that instead of lamps he spent much of his time in the evenings on the Internet on gay porn sites and sites where men could meet each other.

There was one site in particular that he frequented. I tried to access the site to see if I could find him on there but was denied access unless I became a member. So, I checked into membership and learned that I would have to upload photographs of myself, including ones with no shirt on. I could not do this myself without becoming a witness in the case, so I asked a paralegal at my firm if her husband would give me some pictures of himself so I could register as a member using his photos. She thought it would be hilarious.

The next day she reported back that her husband strenuously declined. So, I never got access to the site.

As the ex-father-in-law's deposition was looming, we informed the defense lawyer that he might want to advise his client not to bring his client's wife to the deposition. Gregg and I were not interested in inflicting any unnecessary pain on this woman, and we were trying to be considerate. The lawyer insisted that his client could bring his wife if he wanted to and wanted to know why he should not bring her. We wouldn't tell them what we knew, and we got along with this lawyer well. We just told him to trust that this guy would not want his wife at his deposition.

When we arrived for the deposition, the wife was there. We raised the issue again. She demanded to be present. So, I began the questioning.

At some point in the deposition, I started asking this guy about his evenings in the lamp shop. He denied spending time on the internet and denied a lot of other pertinent questions, so I pulled out some screenshots and his internet activity log. His lawyer objected. We took a break. We explained to the lawyer that we had received a copy of his entire hard drive and we shared with him some of the things we found on that hard drive. He was aghast, appropriately so. We then shared with him the internet activity log and some of the screenshots from some of the sites his client had been visiting. You could almost see the wind going out of the lawyer's sails.

Eventually, the gentleman admitted that he had visited those sites. He also admitted that he had sent the anonymous, defamatory letters. He claimed that he sent them because he was angry at our client for leaving his daughter.

Based on some other documents we found on his hard drive, we knew that wasn't entirely correct. We came to believe that the reason this guy was angry was not because our client had left his daughter, but he was angry because our client had walked out of *his* life. This guy had fallen in love with his own son-in-law and was angry at his son-in-law for leaving *him*.

When we laid this out to this guy's lawyer, the case settled shortly thereafter.

While at Brown & Hagins, I was involved in a case in which one of the partners, David Massey, was litigating a business dispute with a lawyer he didn't get along with very well.

In discovery, David had asked for some documents pursuant to the Rules of Civil Procedure. The opposing lawyer had drug his feet on providing those documents and at his client's deposition when David inquired about the documents, the lawyer took his entire case file and slid it across the table to David and said, "Here, just look through what I've got".

David picked up the file and he and I left the conference room and went up to his office to have a look. We were shocked that the lawyer had actually handed David his entire file, including confidential communications with his client and documents we probably would have never seen in the normal course of discovery.

David made copies of some of these documents in order to use them in the deposition.

When we reconvened the deposition a few minutes later, David attempted to use one of these documents. The lawyer suddenly, and belatedly, realized what he had done. He argued that David could not use the document because it was a privileged document. David argued back that even if it was privileged before, it was no longer because the lawyer had voluntarily disclosed it to him. The lawyer then put on the record of the deposition that he wanted to reassert the attorney-client privilege over every document in his file that was privileged. David laughed at him and finished the deposition. He continued using documents from that file throughout the deposition, and the lawyer comically kept *reasserting* the attorney-client privilege every time David used one of those documents.

In South Carolina, people who are sent to prison for committing a crime can request a review of their case through a proceeding called Post-Conviction Relief or PCR. I was contacted by a victim's advocate in Columbia to inquire about me representing the victim's interests in such a PCR proceeding.

The prisoner had been convicted of raping the victim. Her testimony was that he had raped her in the front seat of a 1984 Camaro. After a rather lengthy trial, the accused was convicted and sentenced to prison.

In his PCR proceeding, he had the services of a lawyer who I had never met. All I could find out about her was that she had recently moved to South Carolina from Texas and that she had some experience in the courtroom. I found out a lot more about her during that trial.

In a PCR proceeding, the prisoner is not permitted to relitigate the facts of the case. He or she is only permitted to make legal arguments about deficiencies in the way the trial was handled. This lawyer, however, decided she was going to relitigate every bit of the case, including the facts. Every time she started to argue about the facts of the case, I would object on behalf of the victim and argue that it was in violation of the rules and case law regarding PCRs and the South Carolina Constitution, which protects crime victims' rights. My argument was essentially that this lawyer wanted to re-victimize my client by making her relive the rape.

The judge agreed and ruled, repeatedly, in my client's favor and instructed the lawyer that she was not to relitigate the facts of the case. The lawyer always acknowledged the court's ruling and then proceeded to try to relitigate the facts of the case.

There were two instances where it reached outrageous proportions.

She called my client to the stand to testify. I sought a ruling from the court that she was not to inquire about the facts of the case, and the judge ruled in my favor. He advised the lawyer as such.

Nevertheless, while my client was on the stand, this lawyer asked the victim to step down from the witness stand to sit in an office chair that the lawyer had placed in the well of the courtroom. The lawyer wanted this woman "to pretend that the chair was the driver seat of the Camaro and demonstrate to the court how she was raped". The lawyer instructed the victim to pretend that she (the lawyer) was the assailant.

I was livid, and so was the judge. He admonished the lawyer

for the umpteenth time to stop litigating the facts of the case. And for the umpteenth time the lawyer said she understood, and then proceeded to do exactly that. She repeatedly instructed my client to come down from the witness stand, sit in the chair, and follow her instructions. It took the judge threatening her with contempt of court for her to finally see that she wasn't going to be able to get away with this. My client was in tears because of the heated back-and-forth between the judge and the lawyers and the prospect that she was going to have to demonstrate how she was raped.

The lawyer finally gave up on this tactic, but we were shocked to learn she had an even more bizarre alternative. She went to her counsel table and pulled out what appeared to be "twenty seven eight-by-ten color glossy photographs with circles and arrows and a paragraph on the back of each one explaining what each one was to be used as evidence"[2] that she had hired a professional photographer to take. In all my years in courtrooms, I never saw anything like them. She had located a 1984 Camaro that was identical to the one in which the rape had occurred. In these photographs, the lawyer had the driver's side door open and she was sitting in the driver seat with

[2] Alice's Restaurant Massacree, Arlo Guthrie, 1967

the seat laid back. They showed her (the lawyer's) adult son climbing into the car on top of his mother simulating what my client said had occurred. The lawyer was trying to show with these photographs that it was not physically possible for the rape to have occurred as the victim said.

When I objected, the judge was visibly angry. I think he was also as shocked as I was about what he was seeing in these photos. He sustained my objection and told the lawyer to put the photos away. It was clear he was done with this lawyer.

At the conclusion of the lawyer's presentation of evidence, the judge denied the relief the prisoner sought in his PCR, and I think he was seriously considering putting the lawyer in jail.

I wish he had.

One of the funniest stories I heard in my career came from a senior member of the Anderson County Bar, Cary Doyle. Someone very close to me had lost her father when she was an infant. All she knew was that he had been shot and killed in a bar fight in Anderson in the early 1960s. This person asked me if I could find out what happened. I started with the Anderson newspaper, searching their microfiche for a story about the shooting. I found some articles about the shooting and was surprised to see that Cary Doyle, then a young lawyer, had represented the accused shooter. I knew Cary and respected him, so I didn't think twice about giving him a call. When I mentioned that I was going to jog his memory about a case he had way back in the early 1960s, I didn't really expect that he would remember anything about it. He asked me what the case was about. I told him why I was inquiring and when I told him the name of the man who was killed in the shooting and he represented, he started laughing. Not just chuckling, but really laughing. It seemed pretty clear to me that he remembered the case. After a few minutes, his response to me was weird.

He said, "David, do you know what an African grey parrot is?" I told him I thought so. He then asked me if I knew how long they live. I did not. He told me they can live for a very long time, about as long as humans. While I was wondering what this had to do with the case, he told me that if he shared the story with me, I had to promise not to tell the person who initiated this inquiry. Reluctantly,

I agreed, because there was no way I was not going to hear this story.

He then proceeded to tell me that in the incident, the father of the person close to me had gotten into an argument with another man in a bar in Anderson County and left the bar to go to his truck to get his gun. As he stepped back into the bar, while he was still in the doorway, the other man, who already had his own gun, shot and killed him. Cary Doyle was appointed to represent the shooter. Cary said he hated the case…hated everything about the case.

While he was involved in the case, his wife had brought home a baby African grey parrot. He told me he came to hate that bird about as much as he hated the case, so he named the bird after the man who was killed in that case, the father of the person close to me. And the bird was still alive almost 4 decades later. We then laughed together for a while.

At the end of our conversation, he told me that I was allowed to share the story with the person close to me if I thought she would not be upset by it.

Every time I saw Cary after that, I asked about the bird, and he just scowled at me.

I got a phone call one day from a victim's advocate in Columbia asking what I had on my calendar the next day. I told her nothing that I couldn't move. She said she needed me in court in Lexington County the next day.

I asked what it was about.

She responded only, "You'll see".

So, the next morning I showed up in court in Lexington. I was running a little late so as I walked in, I gathered that a criminal plea hearing was in process, conducted in front of The Honorable John Few, who is now an associate justice on the South Carolina Supreme Court.

The plea hearing involved a 30something year-old man pleading guilty to sexually assaulting some young girls. The victims were each 14 or 15 years old. The state was alleging that the defendant would impregnate these young girls and then convince them that if they took drugs or alcohol in sufficient quantities it may cause a baby to be born with a birth defect, which would then entitle the girl and the child to Social Security Income. The perpetrator intended to get a portion of that Social Security Income from each girl.

After the state made a proffer of the evidence that it intended to introduce in the event there was to be a trial, the defense had an opportunity to respond.

The defense lawyer began arguing to the judge that these were not sexual assaults because it was consensual sexual relations between people who really cared about each other. She wanted to introduce into evidence what she characterized as "love letters and cards" from these young girls to her client.

I knew instantly why the victim's advocate asked me to be there.

I noticed a man and woman sitting in the gallery right behind the prosecutors and I presumed that they were the parents of one of the girls. As the defense lawyer was arguing about these cards and "love letters," I rose to my feet, walked over to this couple, and whispered, "You don't know me from Adam's housecat, but I'm a lawyer who represents crime victims and I would like to speak on behalf of you and your daughter if you don't mind." The man looked at the woman who shrugged her shoulders, then nodded. He looked back at me and said, "Go for it".

I moved through the bar and objected rather loudly as I was walking towards the counsel tables. I stopped in between the tables only a few feet from the defense lawyer and asked to be heard. Judge Few allowed me to state the grounds for my objection, which were that the State of South Carolina, by statute, says that 14- or 15-year-old girls cannot consent to sex. Therefore, any evidence of "love" or "a relationship" was improper and not admissible.

During my argument, the defense lawyer objected and said, "Your Honor, I don't know who this man is or why he is speaking in my hearing, but I object to it."

Judge Few said to the lawyer, "This court is very familiar with Mr. Flowers and the work that he does. We are going to hear what he has to say."

I finished my objection.

In the end, the judge sustained my objection and did not allow any of the letters or cards to come into evidence.

The defense lawyer indicated that her client was considering withdrawing his pleas.

Judge Few told her that he would be happy to entertain such a motion but seemed to indicate in his tone that it was probably not in the best interests of the defendant to do so.

The defendant and his lawyer then agreed to go forward with the plea hearing, and he received a substantial sentence on each of the charges.

EXHIBIT 7 – CLIENTS

Gregg once told me that practicing law would be fun without clients. Anyone who has ever practiced law knows what he meant…

One of the more interesting cases I handled in my career involved a police officer. He had served eight years on the force and had received many commendations.

One day he was informed by his superior that the department decided to start using pepper gas as a nonlethal weapon. He was further informed that as part of the training before using the pepper gas, he would have to be sprayed in the face with the pepper gas. He refused, saying that being assaulted was not a condition of his employment. His superior ordered him to be sprayed in the face and he again refused. He took the classroom portion of the training, scored 100% on the written examination, and when it came time for him to be sprayed the face, he refused again.

The department took away 10 days of vacation time as a punishment in an attempt to intimidate him into being sprayed. He still refused.

The argument of the department to justify spraying an officer in the face with pepper gas was twofold. First, they said an officer needed to understand what the experience felt like so that they would be more judicious in their use of it. Second, they said that in the event a suspect took the pepper gas from the officer and sprayed the officer with it, the officer needed to know what the experience was like so he or she was better equipped to respond to the situation.

My client did not relent. So, he was fired.

We brought suit for wrongful termination. As the case progressed, we learned that there was no rhyme nor reason in police departments across the country regarding who sprayed as part of training and who did not. My client's stand became known in the law enforcement field and I got a call one day from the television show Dateline. They had heard about my client's position and they wanted to interview him because they were doing a story about law enforcement being sprayed in the face as part of training.

The interview was conducted on the deck at my house. They filmed him walking around the backyard.

In the week before the segment was to air, an officer in another part of South Carolina was blinded when he was sprayed in the face with pepper gas, so they dropped the segment with my client and did a piece on the officer that was blinded.

When we were preparing for the trial, I was working with my client on his direct examination and we got to the part where we needed to talk about what his damages were. He said to me, "David, you know this case is not about money to me."

I understood what he meant but I pointed out that I had taken the case on a contingency fee and had worked on it for almost 2 years and that 33 1/3% of nothing is nothing. I also reminded him that I had advanced a significant amount of money to pay for the costs of the case. I told him that I would like for the jury to award damages so that I could get paid.

He said he understood. So, we finished our preparation for trial.

The next day at trial, I called the chief of the police department as a witness and was quizzing him about their training protocols. I told him I noticed that he had a billy club as part of his gear and I asked him if officers had to be struck with the club during their training. He indicated that they did. I got the chief to concede that when they were striking officers with a billy club during training, the officers were wearing padding and they were not struck in the face or head.

I pointed out that he was also carrying a firearm and asked him if they require the officers to be shot with a gun during their training so they could acquire the training aspects that the department was arguing in the case to be so important. He paused for a while, because I think he understood the inconsistency.

He then said, "If we could acquire a beneficial training aspect without inflicting a mortal wound, I believe it should be part of our training."

The courtroom, including the judge and jury, erupted in laughter. After the laughter died down, I couldn't help myself. So, I said, "I'm sorry I don't think I heard you right, could you say that again?"

Judge Victor Pyle (a great trial judge) interjected and said, "No Flowers, we all heard it the first time. Move on."

I looked at the judge from at an angle in which the jury couldn't see my face and winked at him. He nodded back. The point was made.

Later, when my client was on the stand, he did a great job. That is, until we got to the issue of damages. I said, "Now, let's talk about damages."

He immediately said to me, in front of the jury, "David, as I told you yesterday, this case is not about money to me."

I remember that in that moment I considered asking the judge for a break, so I could take my client out of the hallway and strangle him. I chose to not do that. We finished his examination.

At the end of the trial, the jury found for the plaintiff and awarded him the value of the 10 vacation days that the department had taken from him.

Such are the vagaries of life as a plaintiff's lawyer.

When I first started doing sex abuse cases, I was given an important piece of advice by my supervisor at Ness Motley, Terry Richardson. He told me about the devastating impact that a false allegation might have on someone's life. "Just make sure you're right." I took that to heart and I'm proud to say that throughout my career I was only ever fooled once.

A diminutive woman came to see me one day carrying a two-page document. She told me a story about being raped by a wealthy and prominent businessman in Greenville. She said that she had confronted him about this incident, and he agreed to pay her a sum of money to resolve any claim she might have arising from the assault. He insisted that they sign a written agreement about the payments.

She handed me her copy of the agreement. It had signatures of him and her. The document reflected the agreement exactly as she had described it to me. The man agreed to pay her $7500 in two installments. She told me that he had only made the first payment and refused to make the second. Two things immediately came to my mind: first, it seemed to be a meager amount of money for the nature of the incident, and second, he must be some kind of special stupid to not make the second payment. The document seemed to corroborate her story, so I decided to take the case.

I wrote a letter to the businessman and told him I now represented this lady and that he had made a big mistake by not making the second payment. I indicated that if he wanted to meet and talk about it, I would be happy to do so, but our discussion would be about a lot more than that second installment payment.

I got a call the next day from a lawyer in town who I knew and respected, Steve Henry. He asked if I was busy. I told him I wasn't, so he asked me to come over to his office soon as possible. He didn't tell me what it was about or who he represented, but I went anyway because I was curious.

When I arrived at his office a few minutes later, he invited me into his conference room, where he introduced me to this businessman that I sent the letter to the day before. I had not previously met him. I felt very awkward and Steve asked me to sit down because he wanted to tell me a story.

As I sat, I noticed that the large table in his conference room was covered from one end to the other with canceled checks. As the businessman glared at me, Steve told me that the woman who had come to see me was the businessman's housekeeper. He said the two of them had been involved in an extramarital affair in the past. It had not lasted very long, but it lasted long enough for the woman to collect some evidence that she then used to blackmail him… for years.

The checks were all handwritten and varied in amounts from a few hundred dollars to several thousand dollars. The businessman spoke up to inform me that he'd even bought her a truck.

Apparently, when she found out who I was and the work that I did, she decided she was going to try to get a big check. I was persuaded by the checks that this businessman was telling the truth and that my client was lying. She had endorsed the back of every check on the table, and the signatures appeared to me to match her signature on the written agreement that she had shown to me.

I apologized to him in front of his lawyer and asked for copies of some of the checks. They gave me some and I left.

On the way to my office I called her and told her she needed her to come to my office immediately.

When I arrived at the office, she was already there, with her husband. I figured she thought I had worked some magic and had already gotten her a big check. I suggested the husband might want to wait in the waiting room, but he insisted on being in the room when I spoke with his wife. She insisted as well, stating that he could hear whatever I had to say. I said okay. I showed them to my office, where I told them about my meeting with the lawyer and the businessman. I showed them copies of the checks that I'd been provided. I told her that I would not represent her and that she needed to leave my office immediately.

Her husband flashed anger and accused me of being bought off by the other side, which ignited my temper. Things got very heated very quickly and I told them both if they didn't leave my office immediately, I would call the police.

My landlord heard the disturbance and came into my office. He said we needed to lower our voices. In front of him, I told this couple again they needed to leave immediately, or I was going to call the police.

The husband started talking to the landlord. He cut the gentleman off and said, "If you don't leave, *I* will call the police."

They left and I never heard from them again.

I represented a client in another state who had been severely damaged by incidents which had happened to her when she was a young child. Her psychological injuries were some of the worst I ever had to deal with in my career. I liked her and really wanted to help her, but the laws in that state didn't provide many opportunities for justice for victims of childhood sexual abuse. I worked with her for a number of years and in the end, got her some relief.

During the course of the litigation, something happened which I still can't quite make sense of. Her psychological injuries were so severe that her doctor thought she could benefit from electroconvulsive therapy, or ECT, formerly known as "shock treatment". I did not even know that they still did this in the medical field, but I learned that it is much more refined and sophisticated than what I understood it to be in the past. The early applications of ECT helped her, so her doctor prescribed more.

After I had known her and had been representing her for a couple of years, I went to see her during one of her many hospitalizations for ECT. I had gotten to know her parents, so I went with her father to the hospital. When we got to the floor where she was, we waited at the nurses' desk.

She appeared after a few minutes and went straight to her father and hugged his neck. She then stepped back from her father and asked, "Daddy, who is this?"

He was as surprised as I was by the question. He said "Honey, this is David."

She looked me over very suspiciously and said, "David who?"

He said, "David Flowers, your lawyer."

She looked at her father again and with a puzzled look on her face, said, "Daddy, what are you talking about?"

He got a very concerned look on his face and asked her if she did not remember who I was. She did not. He explained briefly what I had been doing for her and reminded her of the interactions between her and me over the past couple of years.

It became clear that she had no idea who I was, or had any memory of my representation of her, or of the legal proceedings she was involved in. It was one of the few times in my life that I was truly speechless.

Her father handled it pretty well. He then introduced his daughter to me, as if we were meeting for the very first time. She chuckled and looked at me, again very suspiciously.

Over the course of several weeks her father educated her about what I had been doing for her and her family. We talked on the phone several times, but she had no memory of me or what I had been doing for her. Her doctor said that apparently the ECT had fried every memory she had of me.

Thereafter, anytime we were talking, and I said to her, "We talked about this", she would jokingly say, "Was that the first time I knew you? Or the second time I knew you?"

It eventually became a running joke between us and as far as I am aware, she still has no memory of the first two years that we knew each other.

I once had a client who called me one afternoon to thank me for what I had been doing for her and to say goodbye. Not just goodbye in the sense that I was not going to be her lawyer anymore. But goodbye as in a final goodbye... forever. She informed me that she had swallowed a large number of pills.

I asked her to hold on for a second and, using the other line in my office, I called her psychiatrist and told him what she had just said. He told me to keep her on the phone and to keep her talking. I went back to her and did as he told me.

It wasn't long after that when I heard a loud crash in the background. She started screaming because someone was breaking down the door to her apartment. When she saw it was the fire department and the police, she realized what I had done. As the police and the EMTs came into her apartment, she was fighting them. As they were trying to get her on the ground, she was screaming constantly that she was going to sue me and that I had violated the attorney-client privilege. She kept screaming my name so all of them would know who was on the phone with her and she was wanting them to help her turn me into the Bar.

This went on for quite a while.

As they were getting her strapped onto a gurney, her psychiatrist showed up at her apartment and he picked up the phone, which had been laying on the floor the entire time and none of the emergency personnel had noticed. He asked if I was still on the phone. I was.

He thanked me for what I'd done. We chatted for a brief minute and he told me he would be in touch. I didn't sleep much that night. The next day the psychiatrist called to inform me that she was still alive, but that he was going to admit her to the hospital for a while.

Sometimes, legal niceties like attorney/client privilege, which I fully understand and respect, must give way to human decency and the right thing to do.

In my practice, many of my clients had serious mental health issues, so I became knowledgeable about many psychological disorders. I also became knowledgeable about the psychiatric provider community in Charleston. There seemed to be an inordinate number of practitioners there who crossed many lines with their patients. I had many sexual misconduct cases against psychiatrists and therapists there.

One of my clients was referred to a psychiatrist who believed that if you were bottle-fed when you were a baby, you missed out on an important developmental experience. So, she would have her patients suckle at her breasts during their therapy sessions! Male and female patients alike. Fortunately, she was disciplined by the medical board, and I think she no longer practices.

One of the strangest cases I ever worked on was a client who claimed to have multiple personality disorder. I say "claimed" because by the conclusion of the case, I came to believe that she was a fraud. An educated fraud, but a fraud, nonetheless.

The case involved a sexual relationship she had had with her psychiatrist. That case was the source of several stories.

First, she claimed to have seven distinct personalities living in her body (other than the one that the public could see and know). The other "personalities" spent all of their time in a rowboat and would converse with each other about various topics.

Occasionally one of these personalities, or as she referred to them "alters", would "come forward" and take over her body. The "alters" were varied and bizarre. They ranged from a saucy barfly who had no filter on her mouth or her body, to a large male African American slave, with the five others somewhere in between. She would sometimes type out their dialogue in the rowboat and deliver it to me so I "would understand her and her alters better". Sometimes, after she had conversed with one or more of the alters, she would bring that typewritten dialogue to me as well. Some of these dialogues included suggestions and advice about how I should handle her case.

The defendant psychiatrist was a cult-like figure in downtown Charleston. I would describe him, diplomatically, as a megalomaniac with little or no regard for ethics or his patients. His deposition was unlike any I took in my career.

Since he believed he was much smarter than me (and everyone else on the planet), he decided to do everything he could to make my job harder.

When the deposition began, he claimed to not understand pretty much every word in every question I asked. Not only did he claim not to understand basic psychiatric terms, he claimed to not understand everyday words. He would constantly ask me to define my terms. I decided to turn it back on him.

Whenever he asked me to define a term, I told him that I wanted him to tell me *his* understanding of the word or phrase. He would tell me what he understood the word or phrase to mean, and I would then say, "Okay, using your definition of that word, now answer the question."

He continued this silliness and I continued my response. We

were both determined that each of us was not going to let the other prevail in this ridiculousness. We did this for FOUR DAYS! (I hope his lawyer charged him a premium for every single second of it.)

During the deposition he gave an answer that belongs in the pantheon of the most surprising deposition answers in history.

Previously, in my client's deposition, she had testified about an incident where she was at his home one evening and he was making them dinner. She said there was a fire in the fireplace. She had gotten warm, so she took off her sweater and spent most of the evening in just a bra and pants. She described in great detail how, at one point, as he was sitting in a very large overstuffed chair, she had come over and sat on one arm of the chair.

In his deposition, I asked him about this vignette, and was surprised when he acknowledged that it occurred. He did not dispute any aspect of her description of this incident. I was flabbergasted.

So, I asked him if he thought this was unusual.

He said, "Not particularly."

I then asked, "How many times in your career has a female

patient been in your home, with a fire in the fireplace, you making dinner, she takes her sweater off, and she comes to sit on the arm of your easy chair with just her bra on?"

He paused, looked upward as if he was thinking, and then said, "Probably half a dozen."

That same client had shown up for the defendant's deposition with a list of questions that she wanted me to ask. I didn't think this was too much to ask, until I looked at the questions. It was two pages of handwritten questions that had nothing to do with the case.

I asked her what these questions had to do with the case.

She told me they had nothing to do with the case.

So, I asked why she wanted me to ask them.

She informed me that she wanted to get him wondering what we knew. I didn't understand what she meant by that so she went on to describe how she wanted to "mess with his head" and maybe scare him about what we might actually know.

I told her I was not going to ask the questions.

She got angry and demanded that I ask them. She was the wife of a lawyer, so she thought she knew something about litigation. She was under the mistaken belief that I was required to do anything and everything that she instructed me to do.

I told her that I was required to represent her in a zealous and ethical manner, but that I was entitled to make decisions about tactics and strategies, including what questions to ask at a deposition.

She was livid and was adamant that I ask her questions.

I was adamant that I was not going to.

I remember one of the questions being, "How much jewelry have you bought at [a particular jewelry store] in downtown Charleston?"

I asked her what the answer was.

She said she had no idea.

We ended up screaming at each other because she questioned

my professionalism and my commitment to my clients. Shortly after this encounter, and after the defendant's deposition, her husband indicated to my boss that they wanted me replaced on the case.

I was relieved, both physically and mentally.

One of the worst abuse cases I ever handled involved a private elementary/middle school that had hired a teacher who was known throughout the small town to be a pedophile. He had been fired from the local high school for inappropriate sexual conduct with male students. The private school hired him with full knowledge of his sexual interest in children. To what should've been no one's surprise, he molested children at the new school.

At a mediation conference to settle the case, the school had sent as its representative a young attractive woman who was described to me as the "trophy wife" of one of the richest men in town. Their child attended the school. She was the chairperson of the Board of Trustees of the school.

After the lawyers finished their initial presentations on behalf of our respective clients, the mediator asked if anyone else had anything to add.

This chairperson then uttered one of the dumbest and most offensive statements I heard in my career. She looked at my clients, parents of two of the victims, and said, "I just want you all to know that because your sons were molested, my child is now safer at the school and I want you to know how much I appreciate that."

I immediately put my arm around the client who was seated closest to me to hold her in the chair because I knew instinctively that she was about go over the table. As I started to erupt, the defense lawyer stood up, put his arms out and said something as they exited the room very quickly.

The defense lawyer, a man I respect greatly, later came to the room where we were closeted with our clients and offered a personal apology to my clients and asked that they not let it derail the mediation conference.

One of the things that I am most proud of with respect to my career is something that Gregg and I did that was not very common. It evolved over time from some initial, not-well-thought-out ideas to some pretty sophisticated demands. I am talking about demanding and getting nonmonetary concessions in abuse cases.

Most lawyers only demand money to settle cases. One of the ways Gregg and I distinguished ourselves from other lawyers is that we really wanted to try to make the world safer for kids. We would do this by asking our clients what they wanted, other than money, to make sure that what happened to them or their family member would not happen to anyone else. We encouraged them to be creative.

Initially, when we started asking for some of these things, we were told by defendants and defense lawyers, "You're not going to tell us how to run our [insert church, school, youth group, etc.]."

We would always respond with, "That's fine, we'll see you in court."

As we thought more about this, we decided to get defendants to agree to our clients' nonmonetary demands before we would ever even begin to discuss any potential monetary compensation. At first, defendants and their lawyers thought these demands were only bargaining chips that we were putting forth to extract more money. Sometimes, we would spend an entire day trying to persuade other lawyers, even mediators, that the demands were serious, and that they were completely uncoupled from any monetary renumeration.

We were able to demand and obtain for our clients, among other things, new training classes, new screening procedures, firing of employees, having all faculty members of a school read a certain book, a hotline for students, an organization hosting a booth about childhood sexual abuse at a local town festival, an entire board of trustees of a private school resigning and agreeing to never be in the education field ever again, apologies, acknowledgement of wrongdoing, acceptance of responsibility for failures to protect children, and a therapy fund for victims to get help anonymously.

The best example of the impact of this strategy (and frankly, one of my proudest moments as a lawyer) occurred in a molestation case. Gregg and I had asked our clients to come up with a list of nonmonetary demands. They did, and the demands were quite creative.

At the mediation of the case, we explained to the mediator, and the defendant's representatives, that we wanted agreement on all of the nonmonetary demands before we would even begin discussing monetary compensation. None of them thought we were serious. It was a very frustrating day because the defendant and the mediator kept trying to get us to make a monetary demand, and we kept refusing to do so until we had agreement on the other stuff. They thought we were just using the nonmonetary demands as bargaining chips.

Towards the end of the day, the defendant, at the behest of the mediator, started making monetary offers to our clients, substantial monetary offers, which we were ethically obligated to convey to the clients. At every attempt by the defendant to do this, our clients stood firm and said, "We're not talking about that."

Finally, at the end of the day, we were sitting in our room with our clients. I was sitting at the head of the table, Gregg was sitting to my right, and our clients were arrayed down one side of the table beside Gregg. The mediator came into the room and began addressing our clients directly. As he spoke to them, he placed some papers in front of each of them. He began to tell them about the very substantial monetary offer that was laid out on the papers he was giving them.

Gregg and I did not say a word.

Unexpectedly, the client on the end farthest from Gregg, just slid the papers sideways without even looking at what was on them. The next client did the same, and the third client slid all of the papers to Gregg. None of them even looked down at the papers as they slid them. It was a magical moment. When the papers were all in front of Gregg, the mediator stopped his pitch. He was quiet for a moment, then said, "David and Gregg, can I speak to you in the hallway?"

The clients gave us a nod.

In the hallway, the mediator said, "Ok, I get it. I saw what just happened and I am going to convey to the other side what I just saw. Will you come back tomorrow?"

I said, "Nope."

He asked again. I said we had wasted an entire day because the defendant's representatives did not respect our clients and accused us of playing games all day, and we were not going to subject our clients to another day of that.

The mediator said he understood what he just witnessed. He was going to tell the other side that what he saw were clients who were serious about the nonmonetary demands and if they wanted to settle the case, they were going to have to do what we had been saying all along: agree to the nonmonetary demands in full before we even discussed any monetary compensation. He said if we would agree to come back the next day, he was going to keep the other side there that night as long as it took to get them to agree to the nonmonetary demands.

After discussing it with our clients, we agreed to come back the next day.

The defendant agreed to the nonmonetary demands first thing the next morning and then the monetary resolution happened shortly thereafter.

I was never prouder of clients or of being a lawyer as when those decent people, whose lives had been destroyed by the defendant's callous lack of caring for children, slid those papers down the table.

I represented a gentleman who was a long-distance truck driver. On one of his jobs he was in an industrial plant that had an overhead crane. While an employee of the plant was loading a large piece of equipment on the back of his truck with the overhead crane, the employee lost his grip on the control to the crane, which was quite hefty and hung from a heavy wire. It swung like a pendulum and hit my client in the head. He sustained a closed head injury.

These can be very difficult cases because you have to prove what the person was capable of prior to the incident compared to what they're capable of after the incident. In his deposition, the defense lawyer asked my client this very question, "So tell me what you were able to do before the incident that you're no longer able to do."

My client's response surprised me. He said, "I used to be able to tee up a golf ball, and then set another ball on top of that ball.

Then I could take a seven iron and I could hit that bottom ball about 140 yards. The top ball would pop up into the air a little bit. When I finished my follow through on the first swing, and took back my club again, I could hit that second ball 160 yards before it hit the ground." It sounded impressive.

The defense lawyer, someone I knew to be a golfer, seemed impressed. So, he asked, "What else could you do before that you can't do now?"

My client responded, "Nothing that I can think of right now."

Ugh.

I also represented a truck driver who sustained an injury that impaired his ability to retain his commercial driver's license. The defense lawyer, during my client's deposition, was exploring the economic and vocational impact on this man's life, in order to assess the potential damages.

My client testified that he had previously been a member of

the "Million-Mile Club". When he was asked what it took to be a member of the "Million-Mile Club" he said, "You have to drive one million miles in one year, accident free."

That sounded odd to me because I love to drive and have driven all over the United States several times. I never got anywhere close to a million miles in one year. So, while the deposition moved on to other topics, I decided to do the math. I calculated that you would have to drive 19,230.76 miles per week, which is 2747.25 miles per day, or 114.49 mph for an entire year without a single stop for gas, food, or sleep. I figured your bladder might have something to say about that.

The court reporter recording the deposition was a former secretary of mine. She and I were friends. I wrote this mathematical information on a small sheet of paper, leaned across my client, and slid it on the table to the court reporter.

She opened the note and burst out laughing, which disrupted the deposition. She apologized profusely and tried to continue, but every time we made eye contact, she and I would laugh and laugh and laugh. I was trying to maintain a straight face, but I was having a hard time doing so.

The defense lawyer, more than a little annoyed, asked what was going on.

I told him it was nothing, to just move on.

He refused.

I could not tell him what we were laughing about without embarrassing my client and damaging his credibility.

The lawyer demanded to know.

I told him it was none of his business.

He took the position that because it was his deposition that we were interrupting, he had a right to know. He and I got along well, so I suggested we take a break.

During the break I said to him, "Look, I promise I will tell you when the case is over."

Not long after that, the case was settled and, fortunately, the lawyer forgot to ask.

A client and his fiancée came to pick up a settlement check one day in a 1973 Chevrolet long-bed pickup truck that had horizontal stripes along the side in many different colors. Imagine a rainbow that had been flattened out and then glued to the side of a pickup.

After transacting our business, I walked them out onto the front porch of my office. I noticed the truck and commented on it.

My client told me that it was theirs. He also told me that it was haunted.

I said, "Really?"

"Yes," he responded and continued, "it belonged to my fiancée's daddy. Ever since he died, he will not let anyone but her open the driver's side door."

I had no words. I just looked at his fiancée.

She nodded vigorously.

He continued, "Whenever I'm going to drive, I have to get in on the passenger side and slide across the front seat."

I looked at her again.

She nodded again.

He then asked, "You want to check it out?"

I begged off, saying I had to see a man about a dog.

I represented a man who was working on a master's thesis at Clemson University. His thesis was to merely transcribe the letters of an obscure historical figure. While he was working on this project, he learned that two professors in his department were having inappropriate relationships with female students. He brought his concerns about this to a member of the administration. He was encouraged to gather more information, which he did.

After he handed over more information about the conduct of these professors to the administration, the professors caught wind of it. One of them was serving as the temporary department head. He decided to appoint the other professor, his friend and fellow-wrongdoer, to investigate the master's thesis of my client.

They accused him of plagiarism. The department head unilaterally decided to revoke my client's master's degree. Clemson had a well-established procedure for any allegation of academic misconduct. These two professors did not go through the normal process. They just decided to take matters into their own hands.

When I got involved, I was able to get an emergency restraining order against Clemson to stop the school from taking away my client's master's thesis, unless and until they followed their own normal procedures.

As the case progressed, it became apparent that at least with respect to some of the letters he was transcribing, my client had in fact copied work that had already been done and published by a doctoral student at a different university.

The husband of my client's advisor was a scientist at a government laboratory somewhere in the Northeast. Apparently, the scientists at the lab had too much time on their hands because they decided to do a content analysis of the alleged plagiarism. Their conclusions were laughable. They determined that silly mistakes like identically misspelled words and punctuation errors *which appeared identically in both the doctoral student's work and my client's work* were merely coincidental. They even offered to testify at the trial. Pffft.

EXHIBIT 8 – DEFENDANTS

Most of my career was spent representing plaintiffs. This Exhibit contains stories about people that I did not represent, and in most cases, had sued. Being sued is never fun, but it may nonetheless generate some interesting stories…

One of the strangest settlement offers I ever received was from a defendant who offered a used motorcycle to settle the case against him. It wasn't a special edition Harley Davidson; it was a dirt bike. My client expectedly declined. The defendant could not understand why someone would not want his motorcycle. He sent me a very detailed description of the motorcycle and all the things he had done to it over the years and why it was more valuable than my client seemed to understand. He was personally offended that neither my client nor me thought the motorcycle was a reasonable way to settle the case.

I tried to explain to him that if I took 33 1/3% of the motorcycle as my fee, the darn thing would not work for either my client or me.

There was once an associate Bishop in a diocese on Long Island that I unfortunately had dealings with. I say unfortunately because even though he was supposed to be a man of the cloth, he was the meanest, most uncaring, most annoying son-of-a-bitch I ever encountered.

Alan Placa was his name. The case involved multiple victims of a Catholic priest, and I was asked to meet with this "Bishop" to see if we could get them resolved. Early in our first meeting, this "Bishop" began disparaging my clients and minimizing what had been done to them (the abuse was exceedingly horrific). The things he was saying and the way in which he was saying them gave me a very strong sense that this guy was probably a perpetrator himself. I never accused him of that, but it changed the tenor of our discussions.

I really didn't like him. And he really didn't like me. We ended up shouting at each other more than once.

Over the course of a couple years we ended up getting the cases resolved, due in large part to someone else being assigned to work with me to resolve the cases.

I later learned a couple of things about this "Bishop". One of the things I learned was that he was, in fact, a perpetrator. Some men in New York accused him of molesting them when they were young. The diocese took away his faculties, or his ability to act on behalf of the diocese.

And then I learned that he was a lifelong friend of Rudy Giuliani, who asked for special dispensation from the diocese to let this "Bishop" perform sacraments at Giuliani's mother's funeral. I also learned that after he left the church, Giuliani hired him at his "security" firm.

Talk about the fox guarding the hen house…

I was in a settlement conference once with a different Catholic Bishop who spent most our time together poor mouthing and suggesting that my clients really weren't as damaged as they said they were.

I became quite annoyed with this guy. For several hours, he continuously tried to guilt me into lowering our demands. He said my clients were taking money away from the poor that the church could be doing good things with. I'd finally had enough.

I told him that I knew how much money *he* had spent on *his* Christmas party just a few months before (which I really did know), and that it was substantially more than my clients were asking for. I asked why he didn't use *that* money to help the poor.

He was instantly furious at me. He told me that had nothing to do with these cases. I told him, rather loudly, that it had everything to do with him trying to make my clients feel guilty for attempting to get a monetary settlement from the diocese.

We settled all the cases within the hour. It was way more than the total amount that he was offering to all of my clients prior to our little chat.

Early in my career, I was involved in a bizarre case filed in bankruptcy court. I represented a widow who, with her husband, had created and built a successful business, over some forty years, in Greenville, repairing tractor-trailers.

When her husband passed away, she decided to sell the business because it was too much for her to handle alone at her advanced age. She agreed to sell the business to a man who had only recently relocated to Greenville from out of state and said he was looking to buy a business in town. She was impressed by him, thought he was an honest man, and agreed to sell the business to him on a promissory note.

Most of the employees who previously worked for her and her husband stayed on with the business. When this new guy, we'll call him Don, showed up at the business, the employees were not impressed. Over the next several months, substantial assets of the business started disappearing, including a pickup truck and a trailer. When Don was asked about them, he either gave a strange answer or no answer at all.

The employees started contacting my client because they remained loyal to her. One of the employees caught Don cutting sections of heavy-duty copper wire off of a spool and cutting it into small pieces. He then took it to a scrap yard and sold it for scrap. The employees came to a collective realization that this man was bleeding the company. They began to be concerned about the viability of the business and their jobs.

Their worst fears were realized one day when he showed up at the office with a paper sack. He went around to several of the employees showing them the contents of the paper sack. It contained cash… lots of cash. He told some of the employees it was $120,000. He told others it was $200,000. He told all of them he was going to Las Vegas. He went into some detail about how he was going to gamble that cash to try to save the company from bankruptcy. When he returned from Las Vegas the next week, he told the employees that he had not been successful and that he was going to have to file bankruptcy, which he then did.

The employees all lost their jobs. They were very suspicious about this ploy, so they reached out to my client, who was justifiably outraged. She did not believe that Don actually lost this money, so she hired my firm to investigate whether he was committing bankruptcy fraud. I was assigned the case.

I filed what is known as an adversary proceeding in the bankruptcy court alleging that the defendant was either concealing or had transferred substantial assets that should be in the bankruptcy estate. A lawyer that Don hired was very angry at me for making what he referred to as "scurrilous allegations". He argued to me that his client was down on his luck and it was bad enough having to file bankruptcy, but being accused of fraud was over-the-top.

We requested from the bankruptcy trustee permission to go on to the premises of the business, which had not been open for several months. We were granted permission. My client and I spent the entire afternoon walking the premises, looking for clues and searching file cabinets.

One of the things we discovered was a file sitting on a desk that contained phone bills for the company for the past few years. As I perused it, I found the bill which covered the time when Don allegedly went to Las Vegas. He was "bright" enough to call collect every time he called the office, which was daily. So, the numbers from which he called were indicated on this bill.

We were able to quickly determine that several of the calls came from a hotel in Las Vegas. With a few calls, we were also able to determine where all of the other calls came from, except one.

I started calling the number when I got back to my office. The phone would just ring and ring. For the next several days, every time I had some spare time, I would dial this number. On one of these attempts, quite unexpectedly, someone picked up the phone and said, "Brothel". I was so shocked I didn't know what to say, so I hung up.

I then gathered my thoughts and called the number back. No one answered.

For the next several days, I continued trying the number, but I never got an answer. I got frustrated and decided to try a different tact.

The call came from a town in Nevada called Boulder City. I got a legal directory and found there were very few lawyers in that town. I chose one, called, and told him that I was interested in hiring a private investigator and inquired whether he could recommend one. He asked the nature of the matter I was working on. I gave him a brief synopsis of the case and then told him about the phone number that apparently was at a brothel in his town. He asked me for the phone number.

When I jokingly asked him why he wanted it, he told me he was the city attorney for Boulder City and that if there was a brothel operating in that town he wanted to find it because they would shut it down immediately. He told me that even though prostitution is legal in Nevada, it is not legal in most counties and it was definitely not legal in Boulder City. I gave them the phone number.

He called me back in just a few minutes and said, "David this is really weird. That phone number is a payphone at a remote airport out in the middle of the desert, which mostly services aerial tours of the Grand Canyon." It seemed to be a dead end.

A few weeks later, I was driving up I-85 on my way to Winston-Salem, NC to attend a continuing legal education seminar at Wake Forest University. As I was approaching Charlotte, I saw a pickup truck that met the description of the one that used to belong to the company, and that went missing after Don took over the company. He had repeatedly told everyone at the company, *and the bankruptcy court*, that he had no idea where it was. Attached to the pickup truck was a trailer that also fit the description of a trailer that was also missing from the company.

The trailer and the bed of the pickup truck were filled with furniture and household items. As I pulled up alongside of the pickup, there was Don, driving as if he didn't have a care in the world. It was one of those moments when it was hard to argue against Divine Intervention.

I rode alongside him for a minute, and he must've noticed a vehicle doing that, because he finally looked over. When he did, I just smiled, and he recognized me. I then lowered my speed a little and got behind him. I recorded the number of the tag on the trailer and the truck. I followed him for quite a while until he got off the interstate.

I decided not to follow him, recalling the old adage that desperate men do desperate things.

When I arrived in Winston-Salem I called a law school friend of mine who practiced in Charlotte and asked him if he would check the property records in the Charlotte area to see if there had been a purchase of any property either by Don, his wife, or his mother-in-law.

On Monday, my friend reported back there had indeed been a purchase of a lot in a new subdivision by Don's mother-in-law. He gave me the address, so I headed to Charlotte. When I arrived at the address, a large house was being built in a very nice subdivision. It was almost finished.

I approached some of the subcontractors who were working on the house and asked if they knew who owned it. They said they did not, but they had been working with a man named Don.

They answered my questions and I was not very surprised to learn that Don had been paying everyone in cash. I took lots and lots of pictures of the house. I left my card with several of the subcontractors and returned home.

I immediately began filing papers in the bankruptcy court to disclose to the court what I discovered. A few days later, I got a call from one of the subcontractors who told me that Don had been contacting each of them trying to pay them with a check and wanting the cash back, which I found comical.

In the end, Don was charged with a federal crime of

bankruptcy fraud. The Trustee said it was the very first charge of criminal fraud in bankruptcy court in the history of South Carolina. The bankruptcy trustee took possession of the house and all its contents, the pickup truck, the trailer, and other assets present on the property.

Occasionally in the practice of law, one encounters a witness so astonishing, so surprising, that it is hard to comprehend. Doing the type of work I did certainly exposed me to my share of them. Some of them you can read about herein. However, one witness tops all of the others. Berkeley Grimball was the headmaster of Porter-Gaud School from its inception in 1964 until his retirement in 1988. He was one of the administrators who knew he had a pedophile on his staff for more than 10 years yet did nothing to protect students. Nothing.

His deposition was one of the most surreal experiences of my career. If I had written his testimony as fiction, no one would have thought it was possible that anyone could be that cold and callous with respect to the safety of children. The only disagreement Gregg and I had during that litigation was who was going to get to cross-examine this guy at trial. Grimball solved that problem for us by dying before the trial.

Usually deposition testimony at a trial is dry and elicits almost no reaction from the jury. In this case, when Grimball's testimony was read in court, the jury audibly gasped at some of his words. Here are some of the lowlights:

Grimball arrived for the deposition with Porter-Gaud's lawyers. He wore a dark suit and horn-rimmed glasses; his most notable feature was his unnaturally white hair. He was an arrogant member of an old Charleston family who believed, without evidentiary support, that he was superior to most people and could recognize not only other superior people, but especially inferior people. I refused to shake his hand.

We wasted no time. I asked the court reporter to swear him in. She instructed him to raise his right hand and swear to tell the truth, the whole truth, and nothing but the truth. He did so.

The deposition began slowly with him recounting his

educational and professional background. He began teaching in 1945, and was in the education field until 1988, when he retired from Porter-Gaud.

Grimball testified that the pedophile's sexual proposition to a young boy happened in the '80-'81 school year, not 1972 when it actually did occur. He claimed he confronted Eddie Fischer, the pedophile, about it and Fischer denied it.

"I told [Fischer] at that time that if I heard anything more from this parent about his actions with his son, that I would ask for his resignation."

He then testified that "Major" James Bishop "Skip" Alexander came to him toward the end of the school year in 1982 and told him he had received a phone call from a parent alleging, in Grimball's words, that "Fischer had taken his son to his home, Fischer's home, shown him pornographic material and made a pass at him." Grimball said he told Alexander to ask Mr. Fischer to resign. "So, as a result of that, Mr. Fischer resigned, and Mr. Alexander was the one who brought me the letter."

After he acknowledged that the first call in 1972 came from the young boy's father, I asked him more about the call, and if he'd taken notes of the call or put anything in Fischer's personnel file. He said he hadn't.

"It just never occurred to me," he said.

He said he did not talk to the student or do any other investigation beyond asking Fischer about it. I asked why he chose not to ask the student about it.

"Because I felt like that I… my job was to find out from the teacher, the faculty member, who was accused of the… of sexually abusing or becoming… I would say… using the term 'too intimate' with this man's child. I didn't see any point in talking to the student about it."

Grimball's timeline between the two calls was always very curious to us. He maintained that the first call was the academic year before the 1982 call and flatly denied that it could've been ten years before.

I then asked him about the call in 1982.

He testified he did not confront Fischer about this allegation. When I asked why not, he replied, "Because Fischer had been put on probation. I'm trying to make this clear. I'm sorry if I'm not. He was, in a sense, put on probation after the first call, was told that if I heard anything more about it, he'd be asked to resign. So, he knew that. So, he knew he had to resign. Mr. Alexander said, 'Well, he's resigned.'"

I asked a follow-up question, "And once the allegation was made without ascertaining whether it was true or not, you asked for his resignation?"

"Exactly, because I felt that Mr. Alexander had told me that a parent had called. I didn't think a parent would call with an allegation like that if it weren't true."

"What was different about that allegation and the first call you got?"

"The first call that I got had to do with Mr. Fischer allegedly helping this kid with his lessons at a drugstore, a public drugstore, not taking a kid to his house and performing any sex acts on him. There's a big difference."

I asked if he or Alexander did any investigation to ascertain the truth of the new allegation. His reply was interesting. "Because the parent had called. A parent would not make up a story like that and call a school to put his child in that position, or the family in that position, if it weren't true. That's what I assumed."

"Did you contact the police?"

"It didn't occur to me. I mean, it wasn't anything that... for example, I don't know what the laws are now regarding this thing because this has been 10 years since I was even in the school business, so maybe the whole thing has changed. I had no obligation to report anything to police. The way I looked at it at that time, this was a school problem."

"Okay, Mr. Grimball. In 1982, if you witnessed someone breaking into the house across the street from your home, would you call the police?"

"Yes, certainly. The same way right now, if I saw anybody breaking into the house, I would call the police."

"Why would you do that?"

"Because they're breaking the law and breaking into the house, and I see the guy breaking into the house."

"Do you think you have any legal obligation to do that?"

"No."

"But is it fair to say that you would feel some moral compunction to do that?"

"Yes."

"In 1982, did you feel any moral obligation to contact the police about this allegation against Ed Fischer?"

"No."

"Why not?"

"Because, in the first place, this was something that was... it was brought to my attention; an action was taking place in Fischer's house. It was certainly an immoral situation, but I saw no reason to report that situation to the police."

I asked him whether he did anything to find out if Fischer had done similar things to other students. He said he didn't. When I asked him why and suggested in my question that he wanted to protect the school's reputation or was afraid of Fischer suing the school for slander, he got angry and defensive.

"I wasn't afraid of anything. I was doing what I thought was the best thing to do as the headmaster of the school, period, at that time. And it never occurred to me that this whole thing was... I was supposed to notify the students we had a possible pedophile on the staff? I mean, that would be ridiculous."

Grimball then testified that he did not inform other faculty members about why Fischer resigned because "everyone resigns for different reasons". He also admitted that he took no notes of the events surrounding Fischer's resignation and did not put any documentation in Fischer's personnel file. He did not create any document whatsoever related to the resignation.

"Do you think that would be important information for subsequent employers, the reason why a teacher was fired or resigned?"

"I don't think it would have any particular... I don't think any... the successor to my position would have any reason to know why a certain teacher left while I was there."

"While you were at Porter-Gaud or any other school that you worked at, when you were hiring teachers, would it have been important to you to know whether a teacher had resigned from another school because of an allegation of sexual misconduct involving a student?"

"I would like to have that information, yeah."

"What about whoever might follow you as the headmaster of Porter-Gaud? Do you think it would be important for whoever followed you at Porter-Gaud to know that this allegation had been made against a teacher at Porter-Gaud?"

"Not in any written form. If they wanted to know why the teacher left, I would probably tell them." His responses were the quintessential "passing the trash" mentality; it is the pattern and practice in the education field of moving bad teachers from one school to another by giving favorable or neutral recommendations for bad teachers in writing, even those who have demonstrated a sexual interest in children. Nothing negative is stated in writing, usually to avoid a defamation lawsuit by the bad teacher, but if a prospective employer calls the prior employer, they will supposedly provide more information about the teacher orally – but not necessarily the truth. It is a practice that has but one inevitable result: children are put in harm's way.

"Are you comfortable today that your decision not to put anything in Eddie Fischer's file about either of these allegations was the appropriate thing to do?"

"Yes."

"Did you ever tell any parents why Ed Fischer resigned from the school?"

"No."

"Why not, same reason as students and faculty?"

"Nobody asked me about it. I didn't want... I wasn't going to volunteer the information."

"Did you ever tell the board of trustees why Ed Fischer resigned?"

"No."

"Why not?"

"I didn't have to."

"Did you want to?"

"No. It wasn't any of their business."

"It was none of their business that a faculty member had been accused of sexual misconduct with a student at their school?"

"No, I didn't think so."

He acknowledged, surprisingly, that Fischer did not leave the school the same day in 1982 that Alexander told him about the incident and that Fischer had agreed to resign. Fischer was permitted to finish teaching the rest of the school year, about two weeks. Fischer submitted a letter of resignation after the school year ended. I showed Grimball his letter accepting Fischer's resignation. He explained that he wrote a similar letter to everyone who leaves the school for whatever reason.

"So, if I understand what you're saying, you saw the

resignation of Ed Fischer as just a routine matter for the school?"

"Well, it was a resignation, and it wasn't routine because this was the first time we ever had to deal with a sexual allegation brought on by a teacher. It was a different one, obviously. Each one of them is different."

"And even though it was a different reason, you didn't see this resignation as being any different than all the other resignations you had accepted . . ."

"Well, maybe they had different reasons. Some woman is resigning because her husband's being transferred. I mean, there are different reasons for each person leaving an institution or business."

"What did you want to see Eddie Fischer do to make sure that it didn't happen again?"

"Well, I would hope that he would get counseling, psychiatric counseling, whatever these people have to go through to get more or less emotionally cured, away from their sexual proclivities. Obviously, that's what I was referring to."

"Did you ever find out or try to find out if the student

needed any counseling?"

"No."

"Was that important to you?"

"I didn't think it was certainly important enough for me to find out what the student was doing. After all, they've got parents."

Grimball then testified about an English teacher he fired because the teacher would "invite students over to his house and drink beer and tell stories. And that's all he did, and he was warned about it, because my feeling was that that just wasn't the thing to do as a faculty member." He fired the teacher in the middle of the school year yet paid his contract through the end of the year.

I returned to the letter. "Referring back to your letter, 'taking positive steps to insure nothing like it ever happen again', do you think it was a positive step for Eddie Fischer to be employed by another private school?"

"That's their business. No one from any of those schools ever contacted me."

"Did Porter-Gaud take any positive steps to insure that nothing like this incident would ever happen again?"

"No."

"You didn't see it as your responsibility or obligation to do anything to see that nothing like this ever happened to a student again?"

"Not at the time, no."

"What about today?"

"Same, no."

The lawyer for Porter-Gaud asked for a break because he said Grimball was tired.

After the break, Grimball gave what I thought was one of the most incredible answers I had ever heard in a deposition.

"Do you believe today that it was morally the right thing to do, to recommend Ed Fischer to subsequent employers?"

"Yep."

Not "yes" or "no" or "maybe" or "maybe not". There was a pause before the next question because I was truly taken aback by his response.

"Why is it that you allowed Eddie Fischer to resign rather than terminate him?"

"Well, I didn't mean to ruin the guy's career for the rest of his time, assuming that he'd straighten himself out because, otherwise, I mean, his evaluations from the heads of the departments were always positive, his actual work at the school in the academic area and the athletic area." This statement about Fischer's evaluations was false.

"Do you have children, Mr. Grimball?"

"Uh-huh."

"As a parent, would you want to know if a teacher at one of your children's schools had been accused of sexual misconduct?"

"Not particularly, no."

"What about if it was a teacher that taught a class that one of your children attended? Is that some information that you would want to know?"

"Not unless it would... not unless it involved my own children."

"Is it information that would be important to you to ascertain whether it might involve your children?"

"I don't think so."

I then asked him some questions about statements he had made to the press at the time Fischer was arrested. He had indicated in one of those statements that, "There has already been one tragedy related to this."

I asked, "What tragedy were you referring to?"

"Mr. Alexander's suicide."

"Do you believe that the molestation of children is a tragedy?"

"Not like a suicide of, I think, a very fine man."

"Do you think that Skip Alexander's death is the only tragedy related to this whole matter?"

"It's the greatest tragedy."

"What other tragedies do you think have occurred?"

"Nothing occurs to me now."

The deposition droned on for some time after this, and it was mostly the lawyers arguing and fighting about definitions of words and whether certain questions should be answered. One moment above all others captured the pure arrogance that defined Berkeley Grimball. I was asking him about one of the legal documents filed on his behalf. His lawyer instructed Grimball not to answer. While his lawyer was speaking, Grimball leaned back in his chair so he was behind the lawyer and was emphatically shaking his head at me. So, I asked "You were shaking your head. Is that a no?"

His lawyer objected again and instructed him not to answer.

I asked again. "Were you just shaking your head no?"

Grimball said, "Just fluffing up my hair."

"Excuse me?" I was genuinely surprised by the response.

"Fluffing up my hair," he said sarcastically and smiled.

EXHIBIT 9 – WITNESSES

In almost every case, there are witnesses who are not involved in the lawsuit, except to the extent that they have information that is relevant to the issues being litigated. Some of them are cooperative, some are not. Some are even too cooperative! Occasionally, some have to be forced by a judge to give testimony or provide documents. There are few generalizations about witnesses that could withstand scrutiny, but one is they are, collectively, a rich source of stories…

I once deposed the president of a major financial corporation. The guy had resisted being deposed and we had to get the court to intervene to force him to appear for some questions. The atmosphere was pretty tense when I appeared for the deposition.

My first question to him, after he stated his name, was, "Please tell me your educational background, beginning with high school." The guy just erupted, screaming at his lawyer. He berated the lawyer for wasting his time having to appear, and for the "inane questions" I was asking. It was actually quite entertaining. I had no idea why he was screaming at his own lawyer instead of me, but I didn't mind.

After a couple of minutes of full-throated verbal abuse, the guy stormed out of the room. The lawyer was embarrassed, looked at me and just said, "I'll be back". He left the room.

They were gone for about thirty minutes, when the lawyer came back in. He explained to me that the guy had attended college at night and was embarrassed about that. The lawyer asked me if I could just skip over the question about his educational background and get right to the substance of the case. I declined.

I told him that I was not going to let the guy direct me how to conduct his deposition. I also told him that I had attended night school for part of my college experience and instead of being embarrassed about it, I was proud of it. The lawyer pleaded with me. I again declined. He left the room again.

After almost another hour, they both returned and took their seats. The deponent stated where he went to college and further said that he would not state on the record whether he went there in the daytime or nighttime. I laughed at that last part of the response, which made him erupt at his lawyer again because he thought I was laughing *at* him. I told him to calm down, which only made things worse.

The deposition just kept getting more and more contentious because he thought I was looking down on him for going to night school. It was idiotic.

However, I did enjoy pushing his buttons at every opportunity that he provided. His lawyer knew what I was doing, because he was catching the brunt of it, and he didn't like me much after that deposition.

I was hired by five women who worked at a convenience store in Spartanburg County to bring a sexual harassment claim against the business. There was a supervisor who worked at this particular convenience store who was, in common parlance, a disgusting pig.

Most sexual predators are known as preferential offenders, meaning they have a certain age range or body type or race or other identifying features that they look for. Apparently, the only characteristic this man preferred was female. These five women varied greatly in age, appearance, and race. But they all had a very similar story about the things that this supervisor would do and say to them.

He did not possess an ounce of nuance, subtlety, or charm (or simple human decency). He was just filth. One of the many weird things he did was buy lingerie and give it to his female employees as gifts. They told him to stop because they weren't interested in it, but he continued. They just piled them all together in the stock room at the store. When they finally decided to do something about this guy, they went to the stock room got all those boxes with lingerie and brought them to me.

This pig also made the mistake of mentioning to one of his victims that he always bought his wife an identical piece of lingerie whenever he bought something for one of them. So, when it came time to take his deposition, I informed his lawyer that he might want to tell his client's wife not to come to the deposition. As in the other case I mentioned herein, he insisted that his client's wife had a right to attend the deposition. I acknowledged that she could, but suggested that she shouldn't.

When we appeared for the deposition of the pig, his wife was already there seated beside him.

As we entered the room, all of my clients were carrying garment boxes. We got a few weird looks from others in the room, but I'll never forget the look on the pig's face. He knew what was in the boxes.

When I got to the appropriate moment in the deposition, I started asking him about lingerie. He pretended to be surprised about why I would be asking him about lingerie. He denied that he had ever given any of my clients a piece of lingerie. His wife seemed to be the most perplexed in the room about the line of questioning. I gave him several opportunities to admit it. He refused.

So, I turned away from him, picked up one of the garment boxes, turned back around and opened it. The minute I opened that first box, I noticed his wife's face. She recognized the garment. He said he did not recognize it. I also asked him if he bought his wife a similar piece of lingerie every time he bought one for one of his employees. He denied this as well. He claimed to have never seen the nightie that I pulled out of the box. His wife's eyes disagreed.

I reached behind me and got another box. When I opened it, this time I was looking right at his wife. She made eye contact with me. Not a word was said, but I knew that she knew, because it was clear that she recognized that garment as well. I continued through a series of about 12 garments that I had. He denied ever even seeing any of them, which caused an interesting look from his wife almost every time because, apparently, she had worn an identical garment to each of them.

By the time I was finished with him, I was pretty sure that his wife was going to take more than a pound of flesh out of that guy.

Interestingly, during this deposition, because of the subject matter we were dealing with and some of the salty language used, the owner of the convenience store, an elderly and seemingly decent man, turned his chair around so that his back was facing the table and he stared at the wall. I had never seen this behavior before.

At the conclusion of the deposition he asked if I would speak with him and his lawyer privately. I agreed.

The owner expressed to me how disgusted he was at what he

had just heard in the deposition and was sorry that my clients had had to endure what the pig put them through. The owner said that he wanted to settle the case with these ladies, which he did very shortly thereafter.

I was involved in another sexual harassment case in which my clients, six women, only wanted one thing: 15 minutes in a room with the perpetrator, with complete immunity. That's all they wanted. They didn't want a check. They didn't want their jobs changed. They just wanted to beat the hell out of the supervisor who had made their respective lives a living hell. Throughout a day-long mediation, the mediator became increasingly frustrated because he could not persuade the women away from their demand.

Finally, in the face of a public trial, the women relented and settled the case on different terms.

A man sued a golf club in Greenville to get his initiation fee and dues back, some $6,000, because they refused to voluntarily give it back to him. He argued that his wife had recently become pregnant and he would not be able to play golf as much as he thought he should. He wanted them to have sympathy on him and give his money back.

He filed the case in magistrates court. I was asked to defend the country club. Since it was in magistrate's court there was no pretrial discovery.

When we got to the trial, it was trial by ambush. On the morning of the trial, the representative of the country club who I was working with told me that he learned that the plaintiff had recently joined another country club in town, where the dues were approximately $40,000. It seemed that after joining the new club for $40,000 he was just trying to get his $6,000 back from the other club.

The plaintiff took the stand and testified at length about his wife being pregnant and how he wanted to be a good husband, so he was going to give up golf for his wife and their new baby. When it was my turn to cross-examine, I asked him to repeat much of this testimony confirming that the reason he wanted his $6,000 back was because he was not going to be able to play golf because he just wanted to be a good father.

After letting him talk about that as much as he seemed to want to, I asked him, “Do you belong to any other country clubs right now?”

He stared at me for a minute and then look to the judge and asked, “Do I have to answer the question?”

The judge looked confused and said to the man, “Yes, you do”.

When the man looked back at me, I was smiling broadly. I repeated the question. He said that he did indeed belong to a country club. I told him to tell the jury which country club he belonged to now.

He again looked at the judge and said, “I don’t want to answer that question.”

The judge instructed him that he had to answer the question.

When the plaintiff said the name of his current country club to the jury, there were a couple of chuckles, because it was well-known that this was the most expensive country club in Greenville. After he said the name, I asked him how much the initiation fee was to join that country club.

He pled with the judge one more time to not answer the question.

The judge, getting a little annoyed by this point, I'm guessing in part because the guy had already lied in his court, told him sternly to answer.

When the guy said "$40,000", you could see the anger in the jurors' faces from him having wasted all of their time and for lying to them about why he wanted his $6,000 back.

When it came time for the jury to deliberate, they wasted no time in finding for the defendant.

The plaintiff never did invite me to play golf at his new country club.

I wanted to use a psychiatrist as an expert witness in a

professional malpractice case against another psychiatrist who had had a sexual relationship with some of his patients. While the standards have changed over the years in the psychiatric field, it is now prohibited for a psychiatrist to ever enter into a sexual relationship with a patient *or former patient.*

In this case, I was discussing this with the expert witness. I wanted him to say it was never okay for a psychiatrist to ever have sex with a former patient. He was surprised that I would ask him to say such a thing, and when I inquired why, I was surprised by his answer.

He said, “David I can’t say that because many of my colleagues are married to former patients.”

There was a psychiatrist in Charleston who was known to many lawyers as a “testimony whore”. She was known to testify on behalf of doctors who’d been accused of misconduct. She always testified on behalf of doctors, and always testified that the doctor did nothing wrong, regardless of the facts of the case.

She was hired by the defense in a case I brought on behalf of a patient who was sexually assaulted by her therapist. I knew the psychiatrist's reputation and was prepared for her at trial. What I did not know and was not prepared for was that she had treated my client some years before and had given my client's medical file to the defense lawyers without my client's permission, which was unethical and illegal. It made me quite angry.

While I was cross-examining her pretty vigorously right up by the witness stand, I made a point that I wanted to let hang for a moment, so I started walking back to my counsel table to create an awkward pause. The doctor was kind enough to fill the pause for me.

In response to nothing, she blurted out "I'm not crazy, Mr. Flowers".

I couldn't help myself. I responded, "Well that's gonna be for the jury to decide, ma'am".

The jury laughed out loud.

The judge admonished me in front of the jury, but it seemed to have no effect because for the rest of the trial I got plenty of smiles and winks from members of the jury who then returned a verdict for my client.

I am not a fan of chiropractors. I have friends who try to persuade me that I'm wrong, but I can be pretty obstinate.

One of my issues with chiropractors is that they call themselves "doctors" even though they only have a bachelor's degree. I was involved in a trial in which the other side was using a chiropractor as an expert witness.

When it was my turn to cross-examine this chiropractor, I kept referring to him as "mister", not "doctor". He kept correcting me, saying "doctor" every time I said "mister". I would always follow his correction with "whatever". I was purposely using equal parts disdain and sarcasm.

Finally, the judge, Choppy Patterson, instructed me in front of the jury that I was to call him "doctor". I objected and argued that he did not have a doctorate degree, that he only had a bachelor's degree and there was nothing that required me to call him doctor. I mentioned that I have a doctorate degree and if the "doctor" would refer to me as "Doctor Flowers", I would agree to call him "doctor".

The judge told me that I was to follow his instruction to refer to the witness as "doctor". I then started calling the witness "doctor" in a sarcastic manner which drew another rebuke from the judge, so I dropped the sarcasm.

A few minutes later, truly by accident, I called the witness "mister" again. Judge Patterson then gave me the worst tongue lashing I ever received in front of a jury, and he was right to do so.

Doctors don't like to come to court. It is a broad generalization, but it is pretty safe to say also that doctors don't like lawyers. They don't like to be subpoenaed by lawyers, they don't like to be questioned by lawyers, and they certainly don't like to be sued by lawyers. That never really bothered me because I don't care much for doctors.

There are procedures set up between the legal and medical professions in South Carolina regarding depositions of doctors that are intended to lessen the inconvenience to a doctor's practice if that doctor is required to be a witness in a legal case. I represented a person who'd been injured. I needed medical testimony to help the jury understand the nature of the injury and the future effect of the injury, which is testimony that usually only a doctor can provide.

This particular treating physician wanted nothing to do with being hauled into court to testify. I asked nicely. I tried to persuade, cajole, threaten, and he resisted every overture. So, I subpoenaed him to come to court.

When he appeared in the courtroom, I told him that I would get him on and off the stand as efficiently as possible. I also told him that I did not control the courtroom.

As luck would have it, the other side asked the judge to take some of their witnesses out of order which delayed me being able to get the doctor on the stand. He was quite annoyed at me, even though I couldn't do anything about it.

During one of the defense witness' testimony, the doctor just got up and left. A trial subpoena requires a witness to be present in the courtroom, but he apparently didn't care.

When it was time for me to call the doctor as my next witness, I informed the court that he was to be my next witness, but he had left.

The judge asked if I had him under subpoena. I told her that I did and showed her the subpoena. She didn't hesitate. She instructed her staff to call the sheriff. She instructed the sheriff to send a deputy to the doctor's office, put him in handcuffs and bring him to her courtroom. They did.

When he arrived with the deputies shortly thereafter, the judge had him brought straight up in front of the bench where criminal defendants usually stand, and then let him have it.

He tried to explain his impatience and that he was a very busy man, and that he does very important work. That only made the judge angrier, because he used quite a condescending tone.

She pointed out to him that she is quite busy herself and that she does some pretty important work too. She threatened to put him in jail for contempt of court. After letting him stew on that for a while, and listening to him grovel, she relented. She hoped that he got the lesson.

She instructed the deputies to take the handcuffs off of him after he became contrite.

She then instructed me to call my next witness, expecting that witness to be the doctor. I asked to approach the bench and at the bench told her "I can't call this guy now. He's going to punish my client for what just happened."

She understood the dilemma I faced. She then announced the doctor was free to go and was released from his subpoena, which made him visibly angry. I just smiled at him as he left the courtroom.

His office later sent me a bill for his time, including the time he left and went back to his office and the time he was being transported by the deputies. I wrote back to him and said that I was going to forward his bill to the judge. His office called a few days later and told me to ignore the bill.

EXHIBIT 10 – JUDGES

I had the distinct privilege of appearing before many exceptional judges in South Carolina courts, at all levels of the judicial system. It is not an easy job that they do, but the vast majority of them try to do the right thing, even when it is uncomfortable. I always respected the robe, and almost always respected the person wearing it.[3] Judges spend so much time in courtrooms, no collection of trial stories would be complete without mentioning them…

A part-time municipal court judge in the Greenville area was a pretty good friend of mine. I was in his courtroom one morning with my son because of a traffic violation he had received from an automobile accident.

The judge was running late and when he arrived, he saw me sitting in the gallery and motioned for me to follow him. As we entered his chambers, located right behind the bench, he offered me a seat and we started catching up because we hadn't seen each other in a while.

He told me about a family vacation he had recently returned

[3] One notable exception to this is the subject of a future book.

from. I shared with him about a vacation that I'd been on. We chatted about our families, cases, and just caught up with each other. During the conversation we both used some rather colorful language.

After several minutes, he asked what I was doing in his courtroom. I told him I was there because my son had received a traffic violation.

He asked me to tell them about the case.

I did.

He asked me if the opposing party was present.

I told him I didn't know.

He said, "Here's what we're gonna do. If the witnesses are here, I hear the case and make a decision. But if they aren't here, I'll just dismiss it. How about that?"

I told him it sounded good to me.

He instructed me to go back out to the courtroom and he would be on the bench in just a few minutes.

I went back out into the courtroom and sat by my son, who

leaned over and whispered in my ear, "Dad, we could hear every word you two were saying."

I looked at him with a strange look and said I didn't believe him.

He then leaned back in and told me about the judge's vacation using the exact same colorful language the judge had used.

I was stunned and more than a little embarrassed, because apparently everyone in the courtroom heard our entire conversation. I wasn't quite sure how I was going to handle it, but fortunately, as I was thinking, the judge appeared on the bench.

He called my son's case first. He asked if the opposing party was present.

They weren't.

He dismissed the case.

I grabbed my son and got out of there as fast as I could.

Henry Floyd, an outstanding jurist, before he was on the

federal Fourth Circuit Court of Appeals, was a trial judge in Pickens County, South Carolina. I tried a number of cases in front of Judge Floyd and always enjoyed being in his courtroom.

One day he was hearing a Sexually Violent Predator Act case. I was present, representing the interests of the victims. The case involved a former youth minister at a Baptist church in the Greenville area who had molested a number of boys. His prison sentence was coming to an end and the state had filed an action to keep him in custody, alleging that he was a continuing threat to the community.

As part of the state's case, they called two psychiatrists who both testified that the former youth minister met the definition of a pedophile and that he was indeed a threat to children in the community.

The defense lawyer, in an attempt to rebut the state's evidence, presented two other psychiatrists who suggested that with proper supervision, the defendant would not necessarily be a threat. On cross-examination by the state, both of the defense psychiatrists admitted that the defendant met the definition of pedophile, which obviously did not help the defendant's case.

After all of the evidence, even though it was a bench trial, Judge Floyd allowed the lawyers to make a brief closing statement.

The state gave a closing argument that was solid.

When the defense lawyer, a lawyer who knew Judge Floyd very well, started his argument he suggested that there was no evidence before the court that the defendant was a continuing threat to the community and that he could be monitored with appropriate supervision.

Judge Floyd shocked everyone in the courtroom by uncharacteristically erupting, and said to the lawyer, "I had four different psychiatrists testify that this man is a pedophile and you think I'm going to put him on the streets? I don't think so". He granted the relief the state sought, and the former youth minister remained in custody.

While I was with the Ness Motley firm, we filed a class-action lawsuit against a major American corporation in the city where their headquarters was located. The case was assigned to a federal magistrate judge in that city to handle all pretrial matters.

The judge scheduled a conference with the lawyers at the beginning of the case just to get the lay of the land. The litigation was going to be quite complex. At the beginning of the meeting she disclosed to all the lawyers that her father had worked for the defendant corporation his entire career and she wanted to know if anyone had a problem with her handling the case.

Of course, the defense lawyers were already agreeing before she even finished her statement. My co-counsel and I were obviously unnerved by this but didn't (couldn't!) object.

The judge conducted the conference in a normal, professional fashion and, at some point, she said she would like to have a separate meeting with each side so she could get a better understanding of the parameters of the litigation and where we were headed.

She asked the defense lawyers to leave the room first so she could speak with my co-counsel and me. As soon as they exited and the door clicked shut, the judge softened, leaned forward on the table and in a very sincere voice said to us, "Listen, I know it probably bothered you what I said about my father working for [the corporation]. But let me assure you that that company killed my father. My mother believes it and I believe it. You will have no problem with this case in my courtroom."

Toward the end of the same case I got a phone call from the same magistrate judge asking where we stood with regard to settlement. We had been having some serious discussions with the defense about settling the case. The court had denied our attempt to handle the case as a class action, so we ended up representing 240 individual plaintiffs who were former employees of the corporation.

We were getting close to trial and it was going to be a very complex multiweek trial.

The defendant had made a serious offer to settle and a little over 200 of our clients had already agreed to accept the settlement proposal. However, there was a group of our clients who had no interest in settling on any terms. They wanted a public trial. The judge wanted to know if there was anything she could do to facilitate a settlement.

I told the judge that we had made a lot of progress on settlement and most of our clients were interested, but that we had this group of holdouts who only wanted a trial.

She instructed me to have all of those holdouts meet at a restaurant/motel in the town where the plant was on the following Friday night at 8 p.m.

I agreed to do so.

When Friday night came, every one of the people who did not agree to the settlement was in attendance. Many brought their spouses. We gathered in a large meeting room. (During the litigation in this case, we periodically rented either a movie theater or the national guard armory in the town to conduct our client meetings.)

The judge arrived promptly at eight. My co-counsel and I introduced her to our clients. She thanked us for the introduction and excused my co-counsel and me from the room. We were surprised, but left at her direction.

We spent the next three hours with our ears glued to the door from the outside, picking up what little snippets we could of the goings-on in the room. There were times when we did not need to be close to the door because the volume of the judge's voice carried not only through the door, but down the hall.

She began this private session with our clients very calmly and professionally, but by the end of the meeting she was angry, and she wasn't trying to hide it.

Sometime between 11 p.m. and midnight, the judge came through the door, looked at my co-counsel and me and said, "Come with me".

We then followed her through the hallways of the hotel. I remember it being like a maze. She didn't say a word as we walked. Then she opened the door to what we presumed was her room.

As we entered the room, we were surprised to see our opposing counsel sitting in the room. Also present in the room was the judge's secretary, along with a computer and a printer. She informed the defense counsel and us simultaneously that all of the clients in the room had agreed to the settlement.

She then crossed the room and opened the door to a mini refrigerator, which we saw was chock full of beer, and asked if anyone would like a cold beer.

We then spent the next 2 to 3 hours working on a written settlement agreement and she was not letting anyone leave the room until we had completed it, which we did.

I represented a victim in a particularly egregious abuse case in which a police officer in Spartanburg County had sexually molested young boys in his patrol vehicle. I attended his plea hearing, which was held by then Circuit Court Judge Don Beatty, now Chief Justice of the South Carolina Supreme Court.

In that hearing, Judge Beatty sentenced this former officer to two substantial prison terms.

Normally in a criminal plea hearing, in most counties, after a defendant is sentenced, he is made to sit with the other defendants who have already been sentenced, often in the jury box. Because this defendant was a former police officer, he would be receiving special treatment by the prison system. The bailiffs sat him by the court personnel near the judge instead of with the other defendants.

I then left the courtroom.

When I arrived back at my office, there was a message from Judge Beatty's law clerk saying that the judge requested my presence in his courtroom the next morning at 9 a.m. but left no indication what it was about.

The next morning, I dutifully appeared, not having any idea what I was there for.

The former police officer was brought into the courtroom. His lawyers were already there.

Judge Beatty then started addressing the defendant in a tone that I had not heard from him before. Apparently, while this former police officer was sitting by the court personnel the previous day, he thought it would be smart to make fun of the judge who had just sentenced him to prison. He pointed out to the clerk personnel that the judge had failed to state whether his sentences were concurrent or consecutive, and apparently made some derogatory remarks about his opinion of the judge's intelligence.

After Judge Beatty recounted what he had been told by the court personnel, he gave the former officer an opportunity to dispute what he had been told. The man did not dispute what the clerk personnel had relayed to the judge. Judge Beatty then thanked this former police officer, now prisoner, for pointing out that he had not indicated that the sentences were either to be served concurrent or consecutive. Judge Beatty corrected this deficiency by stating that the sentences would be consecutive.

My first appearance in federal court was in front of the Hon. G. Ross Anderson, Jr. in Anderson, South Carolina. Judge Anderson had a well-known, and well-earned, reputation for being very tough on lawyers who were either young or from out-of-state.

The matter we had in his courtroom that day was believed to be so easy to win that my boss let me do the argument.

I didn't get very far into my argument before the judge cut

me off and said, "I don't want to hear about that. I want to know how you can be making that argument when you got that lawyer sitting right there at your table. Your argument is disingenuous."

He chewed on me for quite some time. The motion we were opposing was to dismiss part of the case we had filed. In the middle of his fussing at me, he indicated that he was going to dismiss the *entire* case.

I made the naïve and unwise decision to say to the judge, "Judge, you don't have the authority to do that." BIG mistake!

He became apoplectic. I then received an epic chewing from Judge Anderson in which he not only said he was dismissing the entire case; he invited the opposing out-of-state lawyers to file a motion for sanctions against me and my firm for attempting to mislead the court.

When I tried to speak again, my boss grabbed the back of my coat and pulled me down into my chair and whispered, "Do not say another word."

As we left the courthouse wondering what had set the judge

off so badly, my bosses decided to call a friend of the judge to see what he was so upset about.

As it turned out, the judge thought I worked for Bob Clay, our co-counsel in the case. If I *had* worked for Bob Clay, then the argument I was making to the judge would indeed have been disingenuous. It became clear to us why the judge was so angry.

A few days later, we received the motion filed by the Atlanta firm seeking sanctions, including a request for payment of more than $600,000 in attorneys' fees. It was a debt collection case in which the defendant had already repossessed, or otherwise taken, all of our clients' assets.

When Judge Anderson learned that I did not work for Bob Clay, and that the defense firm had charged their client more than $600,000 pursuing a case in which there was no chance of a recovery, other than a deficiency judgment, he became apoplectic again, but in a different direction.

He then invited my firm to file a sanctions motion against the defendant and its Atlanta lawyers.

Another encounter I had with Judge Anderson involved what was apparently planned to be essentially a ceremonial occasion.

The plaintiff in a wreck case wanted to use a computer simulation to show how the wreck occurred and had a filed a pretrial motion to get approval from the court to do so. Judge Anderson informed us at the beginning of the hearing that it was to be the first time in the history of the federal courts in South Carolina that a computer re-creation of an automobile accident was to be admitted into evidence.

I was representing the defendant.

Judge Anderson had prepared quite a speech about how this was the future of litigation and as long as they complied with existing evidentiary rules, computer simulations were to be admitted in federal courts in South Carolina henceforth.

I informed the judge that we had some objections to the simulation regarding the way the wreck was portrayed. After pointing out that television is a very powerful medium that would carry great weight with the jury, I argued that there were two major problems with the simulation.

An independent witness had testified that he saw a car approaching the intersection from his left at a pretty high rate of speed. At the actual scene of the wreck, there were no hills in any of the quadrants of the intersection. It was very flat land. However, in the simulation, there was a hill that blocked the point of view of this independent witness who said he saw a car approaching from that direction. Our argument was that the plaintiff's firm was trying to diminish the testimony of this witness by creating a hill where there was none.

Our second objection had to do with the impact in the accident itself, a rear end collision. The impact was significant, but no doors opened on the car as a result of the impact and neither the trunk nor the hood released. In the computer simulation, when the plaintiff's car was struck from behind, all four doors flew open and the hood of the car released and raised. We argued that this was not supported by the evidence and it suggested that the impact was more substantial than it really was.

By the time I finished my argument, it was clear that Judge Anderson was pretty annoyed that what he perceived to be a ceremonial motion hearing was turning into a rather nasty fight about the details of the simulation. He said in a rather stern voice, "Either there is a hill there or there is not, and either the doors flew open or they didn't." He went on to say that when he got to the bottom of it, somebody was going to jail.

The case was settled shortly after that hearing.

I did not try many cases in magistrate's court, but the ones that I was involved in always seemed to be entertaining. Many magistrates are not lawyers, and many don't know the law.

In a case involving an employer, and employee, and some allegedly stolen property, an issue that needed to be decided by the jury was whether the employee was an actual employee of the company or an independent contractor. The judge seemed overwhelmed during the trial by some of the legal arguments and issues.

After the closing arguments of counsel, the judge would normally tell the jury what the law in South Carolina was pertaining to the issues in the case, in what is known as a jury charge.

In this particular case, after the closing arguments, the judge said to the jury "I think these lawyers have done a fine job of telling you what the law in South Carolina is, so I don't see any reason for a jury charge in this case. You may now begin your deliberations."

One of the few regrets in my career occurred during a trial in which I had an unexpected and unintended confrontation with a judge that I liked and respected. During the trial, the defense lawyer was attempting to make my client look bad in front of the jury because she had called a lawyer shortly after the incident which was the basis of the lawsuit. The defense lawyer represented a government agency who provided services for a member of my client's family.

When the incident occurred, my client called the agency to ask what she should do, and they connected her with the defense lawyer. *His advice to her was to call a lawyer*, which she did *pursuant to his advice*. On cross-examination, the defense lawyer was making a big deal out of my client calling a lawyer to represent her, so soon after the incident.

On redirect, I asked her to tell the jury who told her to call a lawyer.

The defense lawyer objected and said it was not relevant.

I argued that it was very relevant because he was trying to vilify her for doing exactly what he, himself, had told her to do.

The judge sent the jury out of the courtroom.

As the argument continued, it got rather heated, particularly between the judge and me. At one point I thought the judge was accusing *me* of committing misconduct, and I got quite angry. I started walking towards the bench in an aggressive manner, raising my voice as I went. The judge stood up, took off his robe and threw the robe over the back of his chair. It was as if he was preparing to fight.

I stopped in my tracks and shut my mouth and realized I was

in a place where I should not be, and never intended to be. The judge and I looked at each other for a long time and neither said a word. I think we were both waiting on the other to say something. Finally, the judge said, "Let's take a break."

During the break, the judge sent his clerk into the courtroom to get me. He instructed me to come to his chambers. When I arrived in his chambers, I apologized to the judge for my conduct. I told him I'd lost my cool and acted in an inappropriate manner.

The judge accepted my apology and apologized himself.

We shook hands and put it behind us.

Early in my career, in a case in which I got my first plaintiff's verdict, I was in a situation where I knew I might get homecooked.

The defendant in the case was a lawyer. He was represented by a good friend of his. And they both were good friends of the judge.

The lawyer who was the defendant in the case owned a flea

market at which my client was a vendor, and where she was injured when a garage door fell on her head.

Shortly before the trial, we learned that the defendant had been videotaping my client for more than a year while she was on the premises of the flea market. In response to my discovery requests, the defense produced to me three VHS tapes which contained footage that they thought proved my client was not injured. I didn't think the tapes showed that, so I wasn't bothered by them.

When I arrived in the courtroom to try the case, the front of the defense counsel table was covered with VHS tapes. There must've been 50 or 60 of them. They had only produced the three to me in discovery.

I objected and argued that none of those tapes could come into evidence and that I did not want them on the defense table because it created a misleading impression to the jury that they had a lot of evidence against my client, when they did not. And that is exactly what they were trying to convey.

The judge's ruling was a little odd. He told me that during

lunch I could pull a few random tapes out of the stacks to see what they contained, and we would address the issue after lunch.

The defendant/lawyer asked the judge if he could get his personal tapes out of the stacks.

The judge asked him what he meant. The defendant/lawyer said he had tapes of his family and other stuff (including truck driver training tapes) in the stacks and he didn't want me reviewing those.

His own words proved that the stacks were only there for show.

The judge then ruled that they could only have the three tapes that they had shown me in discovery on the table and all the rest had to be removed.

At the end of the trial, the jury returned a verdict in favor of my client for $50,000, which was substantially more than we expected. The defendant asked the judge to reduce the amount of the verdict, which he had the authority to do. He did.

The following week, I was at a continuing legal education seminar at Hilton Head Island. As I was filling my plate at a buffet table, someone approached me from behind and with their face very close to the back of my head said, "I want you to appeal me and I want you to get me overturned."

I turned around, the judge just shook my hand and walked away.

I did appeal and I did get his reduction overturned.

In the next several years I appeared in front of that judge several times, but not a word was ever spoken about the prior case.

EXHIBIT 11 – APPEALS

An appellate court is not like a trial court in that there is no witness stand, there is no evidence presented, and there is no testimony. It is merely legal arguments made by lawyers for both sides in front of a panel of judges. The United States Supreme Court has nine justices. The South Carolina Supreme Court has five justices. The South Carolina Court of Appeals sits in panels of three. In all of these courts, and all appellate courts across the United States, the procedure is the same. A lawyer will stand at the podium and make a legal argument to support his or her respective side of the case. At any point in that argument, the lawyer may be interrupted by one of the judges who will ask questions. Judges can ask questions at any point, or not ask any questions at all. There are few things more torturous in the practice of law than an appellate argument in which the judges just sit and stare at you. When the judges ask lots of questions, known as an active bench or hot bench, it can be quite engaging and intellectually challenging. Similar to a trial lawyer that has to think on his or her feet, an appellate lawyer needs to be able to do the same, but in a different respect. The colloquy between lawyers and judges on an appellate court usually involves discussion of past cases, or precedents. Much of the argument usually centers around whether past precedents should be respected and followed or overturned for one reason or another.

When I was in law school, I had the invaluable benefit of being trained in appellate arguments by two outstanding professors that I liked and respected very much: David Logan and Charlie Rose. One of the things that stuck with me occurred during a moot court competition. A student on an opposing team tried to use humor and it fell flat.

In our debriefing after the competition, Prof. Logan made the point that it's okay to use humor, but he cautioned to only use it if it works.

I didn't understand what he meant by that, but I came to know over the years exactly what he meant. It's sort of like when Justice Potter Stewart, a justice of the U.S. Supreme Court, said he could not define obscenity, "but I know it when I see it."

My first argument in an appellate court was in the South Carolina Supreme Court during my first year of practicing law.

My firm represented the widow of a man who had owned a liquor store and who was the black sheep of a well-known and well-regarded family in Greenville. All of his siblings were professionals, including doctors and lawyers.

There wasn't much in his estate, but his family chose to fight his widow for every single penny because they didn't like her. They filed claims against his estate that far exceeded the value of what he had left, including a collection of beer steins and a small boat.

The lower courts had split the estate, giving some to the family members and leaving much of it to the widow. The family wasn't satisfied, so they appealed the case.

The family hired an outstanding lawyer who also happened to be the chairman of the Senate Judiciary committee in the state legislature, Sam Stillwell. This was significant because in South Carolina, the legislature elects judges. Therefore, any time your opponent is a member of the judiciary committee, you have an uphill battle, especially if your opponent is the chairman of the committee.

There is a significant difference in the law between a case-in-law and a case-in-equity. The legal definition of each is not important here, but the significance in an appellate court is that if the case being argued is a case-in-law, the appellate court is restricted to only correct legal errors made by the lower court. If it is a case-in-equity, the appellate court can take a look at all of the evidence and form its own conclusions about the evidence, make its own factual findings, and rule in a way that it thinks is appropriate, regardless of the ruling in the lower court. This is called a *de novo* review. Often, whether a case is a case-in-law or a case-in-equity is outcome determinative.

In this particular case, it was pretty clear that was it a case-in-law and therefore the Supreme Court would be limited to only correcting legal errors. My esteemed opponent decided to make the argument in the Supreme Court that our case was a case-in-equity because he wanted the court to disregard the rulings of the lower courts and make its own findings and conclusions.

At the beginning of his argument, Chief Justice Ernest Finney asked him directly, "Now Mr. Stillwell, is this a case-in-law or is this a case-in-equity?"

Stillwell replied, "It is a case-in-equity, Your Honor."

Justice Finney said, "Okay, why?"

Sam went on to give an explanation that was not really on point, but the bulk of his argument was that the court should make its own findings of fact.

When it was our turn to argue, I rose to make my way to the podium. Before I could even lay my notes on the podium, Chief Justice Finney said, "Mr. Flowers, is this is a case-in-law or case-in-equity?"

I said, "It's a case-in-law, Your Honor."

Justice Finney said, "Okay, why?"

I pointed at Sam Stillwell and emphatically said, "Because he thinks it's a case-in-equity. That's why, Your Honor".

That tickled Justice Finney's funny bone to the point where he could not stop laughing and he lowered his head.

I went on to give my argument about why it was a case-in-law, which was extremely difficult because every time Justice Finney raised his head to look at me, as soon as we made eye contact, he would start laughing again and have to lower his head.

I made it through the entire argument entertaining several questions from the other justices.

Justice Finney was not able to utter a single word, because he laughed quietly during my entire argument. When I was finished and ready to sit down, Justice Finney raised his head, thanked me, and then winked at me.

As we were walking to the car a few minutes later my boss was very irritated with me and told me "Don't ever pull a stunt like that again."

The Court of Appeals used to have a judge named Ralph King Anderson. He was a brilliant judge who loved to use big words and impress people with his lexicon. He was always prepared for oral arguments and enjoyed challenging lawyers on their knowledge of the law and certain cases.

Gregg and I had a case on appeal, and for some reason, he let me do the oral argument. I enjoyed doing oral argument in appellate courts. It is a different skill set than trial work.

Judge Anderson was known as an active judge who asked lots of questions, sometimes just to see if the lawyer was familiar with the precedents that were relevant to the case being argued. Other times he used his encyclopedic knowledge of the law to challenge a lawyer on his or her respective position. It was not uncommon for a lawyer at the podium to be embarrassed or even humiliated by Judge Anderson for not being prepared or up to speed on a particular case, but he never did it just to be cruel as some judges do.

While I enjoyed doing appellate work, I was quite nervous about my first appearance before Judge Anderson. As expected, he was quite active and asked a lot of questions. I held my own for a while, until he asked me how the argument that I was making comported with the *Hancock* case.

I was instantly terrified because I had no idea what the *Hancock* case was. Knowing that I couldn't say that out loud to Judge Anderson, I tried a different tactic.

I said, "Your Honor, I apologize to the court, but I took some cold medicine this morning. My head is a little foggy right now. If you would be so kind as to remind me of the facts of the *Hancock* case, I will be happy to discuss it."

Judge Anderson started reciting the facts of the case which involved a young boy who got too close to a steel drum that had a fire in it and his clothes caught on fire.

Fortunately, this jogged my memory, so I was able to respond in an appropriate manner rather than just curling up in a fetal position and giving up.

When the argument ended and after the judges came down from the bench and shook the hands of counsel who made the arguments, a tradition in our Court of Appeals that I like very much, Gregg walked straight up to me and said, "Nice job on the cough medicine, pal".

On another occasion in the Court of Appeals, I was put in an extremely uncomfortable position by my client.

At the conclusion of the argument and after the judges had shaken counsels' hands and turned to leave the courtroom, a gentleman in a suit approached me. He had a legal pad in his hand,

and he asked me for the names of the judges and their respective seats on the bench. I assumed he was a lawyer arguing the next case on the docket and assumed further he was just not familiar with the court or the judges.

I gave him each of the judges' names and where they were sitting on the bench. He thanked me and walked away.

I went and had a brief discussion with my opposing counsel and as I turned to leave the courtroom, I couldn't find my client. So, I walked out of the courthouse and found my client on the steps talking with this gentleman who had asked me about the judges.

As I got close, my client held up his hand with a gesture indicating that he did not want me to approach.

I stopped, but found it very odd. So, I stayed close enough to hear what I could of their conversation. The exact words are not important now, but it was apparent to me that this gentleman who had asked me about the judges was going to attempt to contact one or more of the judges on behalf of my client.

When the gentleman walked away, I went straight to my

client and asked what was going on. Ethical rules prevent me from disclosing exactly what he said, but his words confirmed to me that my suspicion was correct. I admonished him about how inappropriate that sort of thing was, but he assured me he was going to do it anyway.

After we parted, I called Desa Ballard, who I knew to be not only an expert in ethics but someone who knew all of the judges on the Court of Appeals. The bulk of her practice was appellate cases. I explained what had just occurred, relayed my serious concerns, and asked what I should to do. I was concerned that if any inappropriate contact was made that it would not only impact my client's case, but I was concerned that the court might think that I was involved in it, which could be very damaging to any lawyer's career.

She told me she would think about it and get back to me.

What I later learned is that she immediately called one of the judges who was on the panel, a respected jurist named Carol Connor. Without identifying me, Desa explained that she had received a call from one of the lawyers who had appeared at an oral argument that morning. She conveyed the concern that someone may attempt to contact her or another member of the court on behalf of one of the litigants. Judge Connor thanked Desa for the call and asked her to convey to her client her thanks for taking steps to alert the court of the possibility of this conduct.

The court ruled against my client in the case (I think correctly).

I didn't hear any more about the incident until the next time I appeared in the Court of Appeals. As luck would have it, Judge Connor was on the bench for this oral argument. I didn't think that she knew who I was or would've remembered the incident. However, she must have inquired from Desa at some point who the lawyer was who conveyed the concern to her, because at the conclusion of this oral argument as the judges came around the table to shake counsels' hands, Judge Connor not only shook my hand in a very emphatic and weird way, but she said loud enough for the entire courtroom to hear what a pleasure it was to have me back in the Court of Appeals.

It was clear to me that it was her way of thanking me for taking the steps I did to ensure that nothing untoward occurred in the prior case.

EXHIBIT 12 – PRISONS

In my career, I had to visit many prisons. It was never fun, but occasionally, some levity transpired…

I was once appointed to represent the interests of a 10-year-old child who was at the center of a very strange lawsuit filed by an inmate in one of South Carolina's prisons. The child was the product of a very brief encounter between his mother and this man who was incarcerated and had been for many years.

The prisoner had filed a lawsuit asking the court to compel the mother to bring the child to the prison so he could meet the boy and spend some time with him. He wanted to establish a relationship with this child *that he never met.*

The mother had since gotten married. As a result of this lawsuit, she and her husband decided to attempt to terminate the parental rights of this prisoner so that her husband could adopt this child as his own. The husband was the only father this child had ever known.

As part of my due diligence on behalf of this child, I thought

I should go to the prison to meet the prisoner, so I made the appropriate arrangements.

When I arrived at the prison for the meeting, I was surprised to be told that I had to sign a release of liability before I could enter the prison. The corrections officer informed me that in order to enter the prison I would have to give up any rights I may have to sue the state of South Carolina for anything that happened to me in the prison.

I informed the officer that I would not be signing a document like that and I demanded to see this inmate. There was a good bit of back-and-forth, very professionally, because I knew the corrections officer was just doing what they were instructed to do.

When she told me I was not going to be admitted to the prison unless I signed the document, I demanded to see the warden. I talked to a supervisor for a while with the same result. I again demanded to see the warden.

They called the associate warden and put me on the phone with him. He tried to schmooze me and inform me that he was really sorry, but that I was not going to be allowed to enter the prison unless I signed a release of liability.

I told him that I had been appointed by the court to represent the interests of the 10-year-old child and that he was going to have to let me in or he would be answering to a judge. It got rather heated.

He then asked me to pass the phone to the supervisor. I could not hear their conversation but when she hung up the phone, she wrote across the top of the form, "Visitor advised of policy and refused to sign". I took out my own pen and drew a line through that. They finally let me in.

When I got back to my office that afternoon, I called the General Counsel for the Department of Corrections and told him what I had just experienced.

He said he had no idea what I was talking about but that he would make some inquiries and call me back.

While waiting for his call, I started drafting a lawsuit against the Department of Corrections.

The general counsel did call me before the end of the day and informed me that the release of liability had been created by the warden of that particular prison. It was intended for volunteers who came to the prison to see inmates for various purposes like religious services, etc. He said it was not an official Department of Corrections policy or form and that he had corrected the situation and they would not be using the form anymore.

I didn't get to file my lawsuit.

I needed to visit an inmate in prison to serve a lawsuit that I filed against him for what he had done to the four children of his girlfriend. The case did not involve sexual abuse, it was physical torture. He had been sentenced to 30 years.

Before he was incarcerated, he had been told that if he was disabled, he could receive Social Security Income. So, this rocket scientist decided to "disable" himself in order to qualify for this free money. He decided to shoot himself in the leg. He was brilliant enough to use a shotgun to do it. He shot himself above-the-knee and blew his leg off.

I don't know if he ever got the SSI, but when I saw him in his wheelchair in prison, I wanted to hurt him even worse than that shotgun did because of what he had done to those children.

I was on my way to Houston to work on a case when I received a call from a colleague at Ness, Motley, who had heard that I was going to be in Texas for a few days.

He asked if I had time while I was in Texas to do him a favor. He was involved in a case in which a doctor had implanted a "medical device" into some people, mostly women, which had not been approved for this use by the FDA. The device caused devastating injuries to many people. The doctor fled the country to avoid prosecution. A large corporation had been sued by my colleague for its role in this scheme.

The lawsuit alleged that representatives of the corporation knew the doctor was using their product for an illicit purpose. My colleague was trying to prove a connection between the doctor and employees of the corporation, and an even larger corporation that made the raw materials that the device was made from. He had gotten a lead that a former employee of one of the companies was in prison in Texas and he asked if I had time on my trip to go interview this guy.

The prison was in Huntsville, a town about 70 miles north of Houston. I had some extra time in my schedule, so I agreed to help.

I rented a car and drove to the prison on one of the hottest days I can ever remember. I grew up in the Lowcountry of South Carolina, so I am used to hot and humid weather, but the Texas heat on this day was stifling. I called ahead to arrange an interview.

I wore a suit, knowing that prison officials expect that from a lawyer. When I arrived at the prison, I made it through security and discovered that it seemed hotter inside the prison than it was outside. It brought to my mind the Eighth Amendment's prohibition against cruel and unusual punishment, but I surmised that Texas only recognizes some of the *other* amendments to the U.S. Constitution.

I was shown to a visiting room which was surprisingly empty. A guard told me that they were accommodating me outside of normal visitation hours. It was a large room that was divided down the middle by what I can only describe as a U-shaped barrier made out of fine steel mess. The half of the room I was in was the interior of the U, which pushed deep into the other half of the room. Visitors were kept separated from the prisoners by this divider which restricted the inmates to the outer edges of the U.

I took a seat at one of the many available windows. It wasn't hard because all of the windows were available.

I waited and waited and waited.

And I sweated and sweated and sweated.

After about an hour, I asked one of the guards where my guy was. He told me the guy was eating lunch and would be with me soon.

After another lifetime of waiting, a door on the far side of the room opened and the biggest human being I've ever seen came through it. I let an audible chuckle escape because the only thing I knew about this guy, other than that he was a former employee of one of these corporations, was that he and his girlfriend were strippers. They apparently did private shows for bachelor and bachelorette parties. I was laughing because I could not imagine this mountain of a man entertaining anyone by taking his clothes off. And my inability to do so was informed by the fact that he was so large, his jumpsuit was too small for his body. He could not button it in the front of his enormous midsection, which was protruding generously from within. He had long scraggly brown hair and was sweating even more profusely than I was. In one of his giant paws, he held some papers.

When he sat across from me, I explained who I was and why I was there. After I told him about the case and my colleague's request, he just stared at me for a minute and then said, "What?"

I stared at him for a minute and said, "What?"

He responded with, "Who are you again?"

I went through the entire spiel again.

When I finished this time, he said, "Man, I don't know what you're talking about."

I asked if his name was the one I had been given.

He agreed that it was. I asked if he had ever worked for the company that made the devices.

He said no.

I slumped in my seat. We had the wrong guy.

As I started to apologize for bothering him, he cut me off.

"Sir, I thought you were my court-appointed attorney for my appeal."

That explained the papers he brought with him.

I told him I wasn't, and then he slumped (which still left him about two heads taller than me).

As I finished my apology, he asked if I would do him a favor.

I froze.

He just wanted to get a message to his girlfriend that his release date had been changed.

I thought from the jail's perspective that was pretty innocuous, so I agreed to do so.

He also asked if I minded if we sat for a while longer and appeared to be talking about "our case" because where he was going to be sent back to was much hotter, and he found the sauna we were sitting in to be less unpleasant. I obliged him.

Later, as we rose to depart through our respective doors, I remember being grateful that the screen prevented us from shaking hands because I thought it might hurt.

It was a long way back to Houston, and all the way back I could not shake the unsettling thought of him stripping for the enjoyment of others.

At a prison outside of Charlotte, I was scheduled to take the deposition of a serial pedophile that had received a sentence of more than thirty years.

We sued the school where he had been employed as a teacher. The school hired him even though they knew he had been fired from a previous teaching job for molesting students. The new school put some provisions in his contract that they supposedly believed would prevent him from molesting students at their school.

They were delusional.

He molested boys at the school and the school then acted like they had no idea he would do such a thing.

One of the clients I represented was the widow of a man who died an untimely death from cancer. During the husband's final days, the teacher ingratiated himself with this father and mother, saying he would help take care of their two boys after the father died.

Shortly after the dad's passing, the teacher started calling the mother asking to take the oldest of her two sons away from their home on different excursions, including camping trips.

The mother was understandably hesitant because she didn't know this man. So, she called the school and asked about him. The headmistress of the school (who HATED me using that term… so I used it at every opportunity) assured the mother that the teacher was a good guy and a good role model, in spite of the fact that the *headmistress knew of his deviant past* and was one of the people who negotiated the specific terms in his contract for the stated purpose of preventing him from molesting children. One of the terms specifically prohibited him from being alone with any child either in school or away from school. The headmistress never mentioned this term or her knowledge of the teacher's past to the mother.

Tragically, and predictably, the teacher molested that boy (and others).

Aside from the devastation this crime had on the boy and his mother, the mother felt personally betrayed by the headmistress for lying to her. This mother was no withering violet. She was justifiably mad as hell.

The first opportunity after the teacher was arrested that this mother had to be in this headmistress' presence was when we took the pedophile's deposition in prison.

I was running late, so by the time I arrived all of the other lawyers and parties were there. As I entered the guard shack where you have to clear security before being admitted to the prison, I was astonished to see my client face down on the floor yelling her head off with two corrections officers on top of her.

I said rather loudly, "What the hell?!?"

The lieutenant in charge asked me to step outside for a chat.

I told her I wasn't going anywhere until my client was released and someone explained what was going on.

She instructed her officers to release my client.

After assuring myself that my client was okay, I agreed to step outside with the lieutenant.

In the parking lot, the lieutenant said, "Look, I'm sorry. This is all my fault. We knew y'all were coming today and we know what this case is about, so I was aware of how awkward it must be for all of these people to be in such a confined space waiting for you to get here. So, I decided to make small talk by saying how terrible it was and who could ever imagine that a teacher could do such a thing. Well, the head of the school then agreed with me and said, 'Yeah, how could anyone know?', and when she said that, your client screamed 'Fuck you!' and attacked the lady. It was all we could do to separate them. I feel horrible, so I apologize to you and I would appreciate it if you would bring your client out here so I could apologize to her."

I inwardly chuckled, lamenting the fact that I didn't get to see the attack. I told her the story of the case, including the lies that the headmistress told my client.

With big eyes, she said, "Hell, if I had known that, I would have beat on her myself."

I got my client to come outside and the lieutenant gave her a heartfelt apology. My client accepted it and they shared a hug and a laugh about the blows my lady was able to get in before she was tackled. My client also said it was worth being tackled.

Sensing that my client might've enjoyed it a little too much, the lieutenant made her promise not to do it again on the prison grounds.

Reluctantly, my client agreed.

In a prison you hear lots of noises, some expected, some not so much. Yelling and clanging seem to the most common. Different bells and alarms are also fairly commonplace.

During the deposition of a pedophile in prison, an alarm sounded that I had not heard before. It reminded me of a Klaxon horn I heard on a navy ship once during a security breach. The deposition was being conducted with the pedophile handcuffed to a corrections officer who happened to be a sergeant, for safety. I think they wanted to be able to control him if he went after any of the guests (my clients).

In spite of my experience with sounds in prisons, I will never forget the look on the sergeant's face when this alarm sounded. I can only describe it as terror. I immediately stopped the questioning of the prisoner and asked the sergeant if we should be worried.

He didn't answer. He just sat there for a minute, appearing to be going through some vague memory of some training course he took some time in the past. He then rose, uncuffed his wrist and locked the cuff onto the prisoner's chair. He said, "I'll be back". It did not have the light-hearted tinge that it did when Arnold uttered those words.

I was terrified and, from the looks on the other faces in the room, I wasn't the only one.

After several minutes of this alarm blaring, it stopped. About five minutes later, the sergeant returned. He re-cuffed himself to the prisoner and told me to continue.

When I asked what the alarm was about, he sternly told me to continue my deposition.

I did and I never learned what had happened.

In one prison, the lawyers had an unexpected chuckle as we walked past the library. It was a large room that reminded me of a library in any elementary or high school, lots of shelves and lots of books. The wall that separated the library from the hallway we were in was all glass, floor to ceiling. The contingent of lawyers I was with numbered probably ten. As we passed the library, we all took a quick glance and then looked back down at the floor as we walked.

One of the lawyers said, "Look at which section is the largest."

We all looked and noticed that the Romance section outnumbered all the other sections, combined.

After a particular pedophile's deposition was completed, I was walking through the cafeteria to leave the prison. The deposition had been conducted in a meeting room adjoining the cafeteria. The cafeteria had dozens of tables, all arranged in parallel lines, running the length of the room. The room was empty except for one table with about six or eight inmates sitting at it.

The opposing lawyer and I were walking down separate aisles between tables in the same direction toward the exit, but also in the general direction of the prisoners.

All of a sudden, one of the prisoners got up from the table and started making a beeline for my opposing counsel. She saw him coming and stopped.

I saw them and wasn't quite sure what to do. So, I angled over and arrived where she was about the same time the prisoner did.

He stopped and said to both of us, "I know what you were

doing in there and I just want you to know that Eddie Fisher is the reason I became the man I am today."

She and I exhaled simultaneously, and I immediately wondered if the guy understood the irony of what he had just said.

I was in another prison to serve a lawsuit on an inmate who had sexually molested an 11-year-old girl. He had pled guilty and was sentenced to 30 years in prison. At his sentencing hearing, he said to the court that he did do what he was accused of, but that no one was harmed by his conduct.

I could not personally serve the papers on the perp, but a corrections officer could. I made arrangements to see him with an officer who could serve the lawsuit papers. When I arrived at the prison, the corrections officer and I went to a day room. The pedophile arrived at about the same time.

There were already two other prisoners hanging out the room. They were both very, very large men. Those two men happened to be standing near a counter where the officer decided we needed to transact our business, so she told them they needed to step away from the counter. They didn't go too far, and it was obvious they were trying to pay attention to whatever it was that we were there for.

As the corrections officer was filling out the necessary paperwork, she said to me that guys like this perpetrator knew they were probably going to be sued and it was pretty routine for the corrections officers to serve papers on them.

I knew that child molesters do not do well in prison. I also knew that child molesters routinely lie to other inmates about what they were convicted of, in order to avoid any trouble. So, I mentioned to the corrections officer that I agreed this guy knew he was going to get sued, but what was different about him was that he raped an 11-year-old girl and said to the judge at his sentencing hearing that nobody got hurt.

As I said the last part of the sentence, I was looking right at the two big prisoners.

The corrections officer looked up from her paperwork and

said, "What?!?"

So, I availed myself of the opportunity that she provided to repeat myself.

I turned my body so I was facing the two big prisoners and I said in a louder voice while pointing directly at the perpetrator, "Yeah, this guy raped an 11-year-old girl and said in open court that nobody got hurt."

They both looked over at the perpetrator and then looked back at me. They simultaneously nodded their heads and smiled.

I smiled back at them nodded "thank you" and turned back to finish the paperwork.

EXHIBIT 13 – MOVIES

Two of my favorite movies are A Few Good Men and My Cousin Vinnie. A Few Good Men made me proud to be a lawyer and I routinely watched it before a big trial. My Cousin Vinnie is just damn funny. Throughout my career, I looked for opportunities to emulate the main characters of these movies. I was fortunate enough to have a few such opportunities…

In *A Few Good Men*, a private in the U.S. Marine Corps is on the witness stand and is being questioned by Kevin Bacon (the military prosecutor) about where you can find the definition of "Code Red" in various books or documents.

Code Red is a term used in the United States Marine Corps to describe unofficial disciplinary measures carried out by marines in a platoon. Code Red is not found in any standard operating manual. It is a code of unwritten rules similar to the numerous unwritten rules in baseball that you won't find written down anywhere.

Kevin Bacon's character believed that he was harming this witness' credibility on cross-examination because the witness could point to no book or no document to find a definition of Code Red.

He finished his cross-examination of the witness and as he was returning to his counsel table with one of the standard operations manuals for the U.S. Marines in his hand, Tom Cruise passed Kevin Bacon between the counsel tables and grabbed the book out of Kevin Bacon's hand, walked straight up to the witness stand, set it down in front of the witness, and said, "Turn to the page in that book where it tells you where the mess hall is."

The witness chuckles and says that was not in there.

Tom Cruise, looking surprised, says, "You mean to tell me you haven't eaten any meals?"

The marine responded, "No sir, three squares every day."

Tom Cruise looked incredulous, "How could you know where the mess hall was?"

The marine understood the point and said, "Well I just I guess I just followed the crowd at chow time, sir."

It was an artful and effective way to demonstrate that all information needed to do one's job is not always written down.

Kevin Bacon acknowledged it in a very subtle smirk as the witness was leaving the stand. He knew how effective it was.

During the Porter-Gaud litigation, I had an opportunity to emulate this.

At one of the trials, we had an expert witness testify about how inappropriate it was to not put things such as allegations of sexual misconduct in a teacher's personnel file. The expert witness was the superintendent of a public-school district, which differs in some ways from a private school. His school district's policy manual was an exhibit in the trial.

On cross-examination, the defense lawyer placed the school district's policy manual in front of this witness and, as Kevin Bacon's character did, instructed the witness to turn to the page where it required that something be put in a teacher's file when an allegation of sexual misconduct occurred. The lawyer then went on to instruct the witness to turn to the pages in the policy manual that supported other parts of his testimony. There were no policies or instructions that dealt specifically with the allegations of sexual misconduct. For example, there was no *requirement* that anything be put in a personnel file.

As the lawyer concluded his cross-examination and was headed back to his counsel table, I passed him on my way to the witness stand, took the policy manual out of his hand, went straight up to the witness stand, put it in front of the witness, stepped back and instructed him to turn to the page where it says that teachers are not allowed to come to school naked.

There was laughter in the courtroom and the witness stared at me for a moment, and said, "Excuse me?"

I said, "Turn to the page where it says that teachers have to wear clothes to school."

He indicated it was not in there.

I asked, "Are you telling this jury that teachers can come to school naked?"

He then got it and explained that you have to use common sense and that everything necessary to do one's job might not be written down but that doesn't mean you shouldn't do it.

One of my favorite moments in a courtroom was when I got to emulate Vincent Gambini, Joe Pesci's character in *My Cousin Vinny*.

I was involved in a case against a retirement home whose staff was comprised almost entirely of prisoners. You read that correctly: prisoners comprised most of the staff of a county-run retirement home in Greenville County. This bizarre arrangement began in the late 1940s when the retirement home needed help doing landscaping and preparing meals for their residents. They learned that prison labor was pretty darn cheap. So, they entered into a contract with the South Carolina Department of Corrections to provide prisoners to do those chores.

Over the years the "chores" of these prisoners expanded, and by the 1990s they were performing virtually every task at the retirement home, including personal care for the residents like shaving, clothing, feeding, etc. (I could not make this stuff up.)

The prisoners were housed in a building on the retirement

home's grounds and I learned during the case that the retirement home was actually listed as an official Department of Corrections facility by the state of South Carolina. There were 21 prisoners on the grounds during the time of the incident from which the case arose. The prisoners would work during the day, then have a few hours off in the evenings. They were locked into their barracks at 9 p.m. and stayed locked in there until 6 a.m. They usually got off work about 6 p.m. and many of them would then leave the grounds and walk on some adjoining railroad tracks to a section of town where they could buy alcohol and drugs, which they would then take back and enjoy while "locked up" until the next morning.

Tragically, and I think not altogether unexpectedly, one of these prisoners raped one of the elderly residents of the retirement home.

As part of the discovery in the case, we requested the prisoners' files or "warden's jackets" on each of these 21 prisoners. The defense lawyers only provided these files for seven of the prisoners.

I did not make a big deal about this because I had been

persuaded by the defense lawyers, both of whom I knew and respected, that all the prisoners in this program were heavily screened, that they were only petty criminals, and that violent offenders were not even eligible for the program.

One of my many quirks was the night before a trial, I would review my entire file, every single piece of paper, in the event that I had forgotten something or a document that might not have been important at the beginning a case might be seen in a different context later on. As I was doing this the night before we started the trial in this case, I looked at the warden's jackets for the very first time.

I was quite surprised at what I found. I remember it was about midnight, but I called my co-counsel anyway to tell him what I found. He was as surprised as I was.

We decided to set a trap.

The next morning, in our opening statement, my co-counsel did not mention what we knew was in the warden's jackets. He just made much of the fact that these prisoners were employed at the retirement home and he discussed the drugs and alcohol and that they should not have been there.

When it was his turn to address the jury, the lawyer for the Department of Corrections walked right into the trap. He told the jury, as he had been telling me for more than a year, that the prisoners in this program were "the best of the best that the Department of Corrections has to offer". He went on to describe what he contended was a detailed and thorough screening process for these prisoners. He told the jury that violent offenders were not even eligible for the program, so they were screened out early and no violent offenders would be allowed anywhere near this retirement home.

In his opening statement, the lawyer for the retirement home agreed with his colleague's assessment of the program and assured the jury the retirement home would not permit any violent offenders on their premises.

As the trial progressed, we called every single witness that the defense had listed as a witness for them. With respect to some of them, we had some substantive questions to ask them about the case. We had already planned to question them during cross-examination but we decided to put every one of them on the stand during our case and we concluded the examination of each of these witnesses with a few questions about the screening program and about how they allegedly would not allow violent offenders in the program.

Every single one of these witnesses assured the jury that there was no way violent offenders would be permitted in the program, or onto the premises of the retirement home.

We ended each of these examinations with a question about a specific type of crime. For example, we might ask, "You would not allow, for example, a murderer on the premises, would you?" They assured the jury that they would not ever allow a murderer on the premises.

With other witnesses, we used the crimes of armed robbery, manslaughter, and other violent crimes.

We did this for two days.

Finally, on Wednesday afternoon, we sprung the trap.

Unfortunately, we sprung it on the woman who was probably the defense's most likable witness. If they had asked central casting to send them a sweet grandmotherly type, she would've been chosen. She was an employee of the retirement home who had been there for decades and who oversaw the management of the prisoners.

I asked her a lot of questions about the prisoners' accommodations, the alcohol and drugs, their presence on the premises, and the history of the program. She was quite forthcoming and extremely likable. Then I gave her the same series of questions that we asked all of the other witnesses.

"Do you allow violent offenders on the premises?"

She was emphatic. "No way."

"You would not have, for example, a murderer there?"

"Absolutely not!"

"Manslaughter?"

"No way."

"Armed robbery?"

"No."

After getting her to emphatically deny they would ever allow any kind of violent offenders, I walked over to plaintiff's counsel table where my co-counsel handed me the seven warden's jackets. I sensed from the scrambling on the other side of the courtroom those lawyers had not read the warden's jackets either.

I walked up to the witness stand with the stack of files and set them down right in front of the witness. After getting her to talk about what the files were, I opened the first file and said, "Please tell the jury what this prisoner's name is."

She replied with his name.

I then asked her to tell the jury what he was convicted of.

She went ashen and looked up at me.

I was standing right beside her and just like Vincent Gambini said in *My Cousin Vinny*, I smiled and said to her while gesturing toward the jury, "That's okay, they know what you're going to say".

When she said, "Murder", there was an audible gasp in the courtroom.

As I let her response hang in the air for a moment, she asked "May I explain?"

Which provided me my other *My Cousin Vinny* moment. I walked over to our counsel table and I hopped up on it on my butt and I said louder than I probably should have, "I can't wait to hear this."

She explained how this prisoner was convicted when he was a teenager and he had been in prison for more than 20 years and he was a model prisoner and how she had gotten to know him over the years and how she just thought the world of him. She even testified that *she brought this prisoner to her house to wash her car and let him be around her grandchildren.* I let her talk as much as she wanted, which I would not normally do. When she was finished, I asked if she had anything else she would like to say.

She said, "No."

"So, if I understand what you're saying, this man is only on your premises because he was convicted 20 years ago, and he's been a model prisoner for 20 years and that's the reason he's on your premises."

When she agreed, I asked her to reaffirm that there were no other violent offenders on the premises, which she did.

I then asked her, "Now you wouldn't, for example, have another prisoner on your premises who had been convicted of a violent offense as recently as, say, six years ago?"

When she emphatically said no, I hopped off the table, walked up to the witness stand, closed that first file, set it to one side, opened the next file and asked her to tell the jury what that man's name was.

After she did, I said, "Tell the jury what he was convicted of".

She hesitated, but then said, "Manslaughter".

I said, "Tell the jury how long ago he was convicted".

She said, "Six years".

This time there was laughter in the courtroom.

She tried another futile explanation, but I cut her off.

I opened the next file, got her to tell the jury what he was convicted of, and then the next one and then the next one.

Of the seven wardens jackets we were provided, six of them were violent offenders.

During this exercise, from my angle with my back to the jury, I could see the judge, now South Carolina Supreme Court Associate Justice John Kittredge, had backed his chair up away from the bench and was bent over so the people in the courtroom could not see how hard he was laughing. I will never forget his back bouncing up and down as he guffawed silently.

At the conclusion of this cross-examination, he instructed the lawyers to meet him in his chambers where he "suggested" to the defense lawyers they were going to settle the case that night.

The case was settled.

Another movie I inadvertently brushed with was *Erin Brockovich*.

Gregg and I had a case in Georgetown, South Carolina which involved a 27-mile-long canal. We thought it would help the jury understand our case better if we had aerial photographs of the entire canal.

One day we went to the county government office where we could obtain such pictures. We brought along a paralegal that Gregg had employed for a brief period of time. She was very capable, and she was also quite attractive. While that is not, and should not be, part of the job description for any position in the legal or any other field, it is relevant to this story.

When Gregg and I went into the building to try to get the photographs, she stayed outside, returning some phone calls. The young man in the office was pleasant but didn't seem too interested in helping us. We tried to explain to him why the photographs were important and why we needed them on fairly short notice.

He expressed some empathy and told us how swamped he was and how difficult it would be for him to get us any photographs in the next several days.

We didn't seem to have any choice but to fill out the appropriate forms.

He promised to get us photographs as quickly as he could.

As we walked outside with no photographs, the paralegal was surprised. Gregg related what happened in the office to her.

She said, "Tell me exactly what you need".

We gave her the list of photos we were seeking.

She said to us, "Go get lunch or a beer, I don't care. I'll see you in a bit."

We did as we were instructed.

She showed up a little more than an hour later with every photo we needed.

EXHIBIT 14 – MENS ROOMS

Oddly, the men's room was the scene of several encounters that merit inclusion here…

The first involved a rather tangled case wherein the department head of one of the academic departments at my *alma mater*, Clemson University, sued one of his colleagues, who happened to be a good friend of mine. My friend and one of his colleagues had written a memo critical of the department head on a variety of topics.

It had been the custom of this department to rotate the chairmanship every couple of years, but the current head had already been in the chair for several years and many of the faculty wanted a change in leadership. The memo had been circulated in the department and was debated.

One day, the dean of the college, who was thoroughly exhausted by the endless controversy in this particular department, decided to hold a secret vote of the faculty members to see if they desired a new chair of the department. The sitting head of the department lost the vote.

Shortly thereafter, someone anonymously sent the memo to the *Charlotte Observer*, which ran a story about it. The gist of the story was that the department head was being discriminated against because of his religious views, which he wore on his sleeve and pushed onto his students. So, the department head decided to sue my friend for defamation of character, alleging that my friend sent the memo to the newspaper.

I was asked to get involved and I did.

It seemed clear that someone in the department had sent it. My friend denied sending the memo and I knew him well enough to believe him.

The department was acrimoniously divided between the supporters of the outgoing chairman and those who were opposed and wanted new leadership. As the case developed, I began to get a sneaking suspicion that I could prove who sent the memo to the newspaper.

During a break in a deposition at my office, I was in the men's room doing what men do there, when the department head's lawyer sidled up to the urinal right next to me. Neither of us said anything for a few seconds and then I decided to break that most sacred unwritten rule of the men's room and I spoke to him.

"I know who sent the memo."

He seemed simultaneously annoyed that I was speaking to him at that moment and surprised by what I said. "Who?" he asked.

"Your guy," I said and smiled.

I had come to believe that the plaintiff had sent the memo in order to get press attention, which he loved, and to set himself up as a martyr.

"You're crazy," he told me.

He finished his business, and as he walked away, I said, "I can prove it."

Within days of that brief exchange, the plaintiff dismissed his case.

One of the partners at Brown & Hagins, David Massey, had

an interesting encounter with an opposing party in the men's room, who should go down as one of the dumbest litigants in legal history.

David was deposing the opposing party and was boring in on a particular detail that was critical to the case. The deponent was being evasive in such a way that made David feel he was close to something, so he kept at it.

Things got pretty tense, so the opposing lawyer asked for a break.

During the break, David and the deponent found themselves at adjacent stalls in the men's room.

With no prompting from David, the opposing party said, "Man, you were so close to what you wanted. If you had just asked me [X], you would've gotten it."

David just smiled at the guy, finished his business, and left the men's room.

Back in the conference room, when the deposition was resumed, David proceeded to ask the guy [X].

The deponent, in a rather loud voice said, "You can't ask me that! I told you that off the record!"

A case involving an Episcopal priest, who was a particularly heinous sexual offender, provided one of the more colorful and unexpected moments of my career.

This priest was sexually attracted to grown men, grown women, and children. He was one of the worst monsters I ever encountered. Among the many bizarre behaviors that he was known for was he gave out bracelets to many people in the small town where he lived. They were simple, unadorned thin leather bracelets that he had custom-made, with two snaps. One of the snaps was at one end of the bracelet and was intended to go around a person's wrist. The other snap was intended to make a smaller loop around the base of a penis. It was what some call a 'cock ring'. The priest had given out many of these as gifts.

I was given a few of these as evidence by some of the victims in the town. At the priest's deposition, I brought one of these bracelets in a Ziploc bag. I asked the priest what it was.

He testified that it was a bracelet. He acknowledged that he had had them made and that he gave them out as gifts.

I asked him about the other snap.

He said he had no idea what it was for, even though he still agreed that he had designed them and had them custom made.

I pressed him on the issue and asked him if it was a sexual item and he seemed aghast that I would suggest such a thing.

We moved on to another topic.

A few minutes later, I noticed one of the defense lawyers down the table had opened the Ziploc bag and was snapping and unsnapping the bracelet using both the larger loop and smaller loop. I thought it was a little weird, but I didn't say anything.

During the next break in the deposition, I was in the bathroom. As I was finishing my business and washing my hands, this lawyer came busting into the bathroom, made a beeline for the sink and started vigorously scrubbing his hands.

I started laughing out loud because he and I both knew that he had no idea where that "bracelet" had been before.

Apparently, he said something on his way to the bathroom because the other lawyers in the case all came into the bathroom and were giving him quite a hard time about where it might've been.

EXHIBIT 15 – MISCELLANEOUS

A few stories either didn't seem to fit in any of the above categories, or fit more than one, so I chose to separate them out here…

I was involved in a situation where I was first up for trial on two separate professional misconduct cases in two separate counties, Williamsburg County and Charleston County, on the same day. I was co-counsel with Desa Ballard in the Charleston case. I was trying the case in Kingstree by myself. I explained my dilemma to both judges, but neither would agree to postpone the trial on their respective dockets.

Desa and I had to be creative.

I anticipated that the case in Kingstree would take less than two days to complete. The Charleston case was expected to last for a week. The case in Kingstree was a sexual misconduct case against a gynecologist. The Charleston case was a sexual misconduct case against a therapist.

What we decided to do was Desa would begin the case in Charleston with the opening statement and the first couple of witnesses. I would try the case in Kingstree as quickly as I could and then skedaddle to Charleston.

As Gen. Eisenhower once said, "A plan is only good until the first shot is fired".

During my opening statement in Kingstree on that Monday morning, I was interrupted by the judge, who said I had an emergency phone call from a judge in Charleston.

I asked him if he wanted me to continue the opening statement.

He said no and he let me use the phone in his chambers. I called the judge in Charleston, The Honorable Tommy Hughston, who informed me that Desa had had a family medical emergency and had to leave Charleston after they had picked the jury. He wanted to know how quickly I could get to Charleston.

I explained to him that I was in the middle of my opening statement. I thought it best if the judges got together on the phone, so I asked both of their permission to put Judge Hughston on speakerphone.

The judges worked out a plan whereby we would expedite the trial in Kingstree and as soon as the judge charged the jury, I would leave Kingstree, and get to Charleston as quickly as I could.

I went back into the courtroom and finished my opening statement. We were able to conclude the trial in Kingstree in a day.

I then drove like a banshee to Charleston where the judge, jury, and my opposing counsel, Rutledge Young, were awaiting my arrival. When I got to the courthouse, we immediately began presenting our opening statements.

At some point, Judge Hughston received a message from the trial judge in Kingstree that the jury there had rendered a defense verdict.

The trial in Charleston went much better from the plaintiff's perspective. I got the defendant therapist to acknowledge that her conduct was inappropriate. So, on Friday, at the end of all the evidence, I moved for a directed verdict for the plaintiff on the issue of liability. I didn't really expect it to be granted, and I was surprised when Judge Hughston granted it. The only issue he submitted to the jury was damages.

I knew that if the jury returned a substantial damage award, not only would the case be appealed, it would likely be overturned.

The jury awarded a rather nominal amount.

I got a call one morning from a crime victim's advocate in Spartanburg County who wanted to know if I was able to attend a hearing that afternoon on behalf of a victim of domestic violence. My calendar was free, but I had to go home and put a suit on.

I arrived in Spartanburg just in time for the hearing. On my way to the courthouse, the advocate brought me up to speed about the case.

The accused was a police officer in the upstate. The allegations were that he had assaulted his wife and young son. The wife was requesting an emergency protection order. One of her concerns was that her husband had recently purchased an assault rifle and a large amount of ammunition online.

When I got to the hearing, the accused and his lawyer were agreeable to a protection order. I asked to approach the bench to have a discussion between lawyers and the judge about this assault rifle and ammunition.

The judge expressed some concern about leaving such a weapon in the defendant's possession for the immediate future and inquired from the defense lawyer if he had any other firearms. After consulting with her client, the lawyer informed the judge that the defendant had 17 firearms. Most of them were rifles or shotguns and two or three of them were pistols.

The judge indicated that as a condition of the protection order, he was ordering that the accused would have to surrender all of his firearms. The question then became what we were going to do with them.

The defense lawyer declined to take possession of them. The prosecutor did as well.

The judge looked at me and said, "You're the one who wanted him to give up the weapons, why don't you take them?"

As I started to object, the judge just started shaking his head and I understood what that meant. So, I stopped talking.

The judge ordered me to take possession of all of the accused's firearms. I met with him and his lawyer that afternoon and took possession of all of the guns and some ammunition. Not knowing what else to do with them, I took them to my office and put them in my closet.

As the case progressed, there came a point where I no longer needed to be involved. Legal Aid of Spartanburg agreed to take over representation of the wife and son, which I was grateful for. However, along with the case came the guns. So, I had to transfer all these guns to the Legal Aid office in Spartanburg.

I naïvely loaded them all up in my car and drove to Spartanburg. I guess it was when I couldn't find a parking place near the Legal Aid office that I realized I was going to have to make several trips up and down Main Street in Spartanburg with a whole bunch of guns in my hands.

I found a parking place about two blocks from their office.

As I got out of the car wondering how I was going to do this, a Spartanburg police officer on a bicycle rode nearby. I shouted to get her attention.

She came over and approached me very cautiously. When she got near enough, I started explaining my situation. I was actually expecting a chuckle, but I got the opposite.

She moved further away from me and asked me where the guns were.

I told they were in the front seat of my Jeep.

She asked me to give her a minute. She called in to the dispatcher to explain that she was going to be escorting me on Main Street carrying many guns.

As I recall, it took four or five trips to carry all these guns to the office. The police officer not only didn't offer to help carry them, she escorted me by walking about 10 feet behind me on each trip.

While I was at the Brown & Hagins law firm, I came back

from a hearing one day and was met with a stern look and not very pleasant attitude from the receptionist, Lisa. She had always been a very pleasant person and I've never seen this side of her. She handed me my phone messages and was very terse in her comments to me.

As I walked through the building and up to my office, all of the staff members were giving me hard looks. I had no idea what was going on, but it seemed to me there must've been some trouble in the office among the staff while I was gone.

As I approached my office, I said hi to my secretary, Karen, who just stared back at me and didn't say a word. I thought it was weird, but I went on into my office, and as I was setting down my briefcase and taking off my jacket, Karen came into my office and closed the door behind her. She stayed right at the door and said to me, "Is there anything you want to tell me?"

I looked at her and said, "About what?"

She said, "You got anything going on your life that you need to tell me about?"

I really had no idea what she was talking about, so I asked her again what she was talking about.

She got a hard look on her face and said, "Paternity test?"

I said, "What?"

She then told me that I got a phone call while I was gone from a lawyer named Ken Carlson. Apparently, Mr. Carlson told her that he represented a woman who had a child. They had had a paternity test done and I was the father of the child.

As she was telling me this, she handed me a phone message that had the name Ken Carlson and his phone number. I started laughing as she was telling me the story. That only seemed to make her angrier. So, I played along for a couple minutes, and then I couldn't hold it in anymore.

Ken Carlson was my best friend from law school. He had called to talk to me about something and when he discovered that I was not in the office, he decided to play a joke.

Karen was so relieved when she heard this. She left my office to tell all the other ladies that it was not true. They all had quite a laugh about it, as did I.

I called Ken and congratulated him on his practical joke and told him that it worked. But I immediately started plotting my revenge.

I waited a few weeks. I called Ken's office one day when I knew he was not in. The message I left with his receptionist was, "Tell him that my test came back positive and that he needs to be tested as soon as possible." I hung up the phone.

There were several occasions during my career in which it was very difficult to argue against Divine Intervention. On one occasion, I was in the city of Asheville early one morning preparing to take the deposition of a bishop in a case involving priest abuse.

My client and his father were staying in the hotel room directly across the hall from mine. As I was getting my battle armor on, the phone in my room rang. It was my client's father.

He insisted that I come across the hall immediately.

So, I hurried over, half dressed.

As they opened the door, I could see that both of them were weeping. I asked what was wrong and the father just pointed at the sliding glass door.

As I walked over to the door, I saw the most extraordinary sight. A brilliant rainbow was actually touching down in the parking lot of the hotel. My clients were certain this was a sign from God that he was on their side.

I remember thinking, "I wonder what the bishop would have to say about that."

In the same case, there was another occurrence that beggars belief. I amassed a pretty good amount of evidence against the pedophile priest, but a lot of it was hearsay and uncorroborated.

I got a call one day from a woman who was weeping. She said she heard about the litigation and she wanted to help. She told me that she and her husband had been in a sexual relationship with the priest, but that her husband and the priest had run off together.

Of course, this scorned woman had my attention. She went

on to describe a trove of letters she and her husband had received from the priest over a number of years that were quite graphic and, frankly, disgusting.

I was able to authenticate the handwriting of the priest, and thereafter it was difficult for the diocese to deny that their priest was a monster.

CLOSING ARGUMENT

There you have it, ladies and gentlemen, the wacky parts of the legal chapter of my life's work. They comprise my contribution to the premise in Lee Plumblee's assertion in his Foreword that trial lawyers love to tell stories, and some of them might be worth listening to.

I hope you enjoyed these stories.

More to come... from the road.

ABOUT THE AUTHOR

David Flowers is a recovering attorney who spent most of his career representing victims of sexual abuse in civil litigation. He also represented crime victims, *pro bono,* in criminal proceedings to ensure their constitutional rights were protected. He no longer practices law.

He lives on the road with Natali.

He can be reached at davidflowersauthor@gmail.com.

Made in the USA
Columbia, SC
28 September 2020